Quenched

Christ's Living Water for a Thirsty Soul

BY

DONNA PYLE

CONCORDIA PUBLISHING HOUSE · SAINT LOUIS

Published by Concordia Publishing House
3558 S. Jefferson Avenue, St. Louis, MO 63118-3968
1-800-325-3040 • www.cph.org

Text © 2014 Donna Pyle

Cover photo: © iStockphoto.com

Manufactured in the United States of America

Library of Congress Cataloging-in-Publication Data
Pyle, Donna.
    Quenched by Christ : living water for a thirsty soul / by Donna Pyle.
        pages cm
    Includes bibliographical references.
    ISBN 978-0-7586-4667-5
    1. Christian life. I. Title.
    BV4501.3.P95 2014
    248.4--dc23
                            2014013818

1 2 3 4 5 6 7 8 9 10   23 22 21 20 19 18 17 16 15 14

TABLE OF CONTENTS

JESUS

You faithfully pour Your grace into my life.

Your blessings leave me breathless.

Your strength gives me courage.

Your Word transforms my heart.

Your love leaves me UNDONE.

Thank You, wonderful Savior

PROLOGUE

S o there I was. At the front door. Vulnerable. Ready to bolt.
I was lurking outside of a church I had never set foot
in before. I glanced behind me, my eyes darting back and forth.
Feeling abandoned.

Panic rising.

Clenching my hands together to keep them from trembling,
I focused on the colorful flowers waving from the beds along the
walkway. Perfectly manicured. *Like the Church People inside*, I
imagined.

The night before, I had met a nice gentleman at a club where
we danced and talked until the wee hours. Before parting ways to
head home, he invited me to his church the next morning.

Just like that.

Out of the blue.

I wanted to see him again, but I felt irritated. Ambushed. *What
was a Christian doing in a* bar *anyway?*

The October wind blew cool across my heated face as I paced.
I was scared but didn't understand why. Wasn't God supposed to

be good and loving? There's no safer place than church, right? *So how come I feel so raw? so exposed?*

Maybe because I was, at twenty-two, spiritually lost. Self-indulgent. Entitled to it all. Although I worked two jobs, I had amassed a black hole of debt.

Overwhelmed and in over my head.

That was how I felt that morning. I had wrecked my closet to find something Christian-looking to wear. My simple goal was to blend in. And as I stood ready to walk inside the church, I hoped that maybe the Church People wouldn't notice my stains or see my tarnished past if I hid them well enough under Church Clothes.

But somehow I knew God could still see them.

Disgusted, I jerked around to leave, almost knocking down an elderly couple. They smiled, confusion widening their eyes. But they welcomed me warmly and held the door open, inviting me inside.

Well, here goes nothing.

I do not remember the couple's names, but I'll never forget how their kindness diminished my fear for those brief moments. Several other people smiled their good mornings. My guard lowered slightly.

My friend showed up right on time and escorted me to a nondescript wooden pew somewhere in the middle of the sanctuary. A thundering organ perched in the balcony began the service, and I made sure to stand and sit when appropriate. Messing up and sticking out was not an option in my mind. *Maybe they'll think I belong.*

The organ's low notes tickled my toes as the people sang unfamiliar hymns with gusto. They were all dressed so nicely. Everything all tucked in correctly, even as I kept trying to tuck in my sins like a wayward dress slip. *When they figure out I don't really buy into all of this, will they throw me out?*

Settling in for the sermon, I saw people opening note pads and Bibles, and I noticed the big wooden cross that hung alone over the altar. I don't remember a single word the pastor spoke. I was too preoccupied, masking anxiety. Hiding worry. Shoving down fear.

I survived the service, smiling at the Church People who introduced themselves. I enjoyed lunch afterward with the gentleman who invited me. We committed to begin dating that day. Soon, church followed by lunch became our Sunday routine.

By the time I was baptized six months later, I was an expert chameleon. Camouflaging a heart that was far from Christ, I jumped through the outward hoops of religion. People talked about having a personal relationship with Christ, but the concept was completely alien to me. *Building a relationship with thin air settled at the bottom of my to-do list.*

I simply wanted to be the poster child for a redeemed life. To be the example. To make everyone want to be me. Talk well about me. To look good for my boyfriend and his family.

I received people's enthusiastic congratulations the day I was baptized, but I felt no different after it happened. No lightning bolt of goodness struck me to change my selfish thought patterns or bad habits. And a few days later, I wondered, *Isn't life supposed to immediately improve when someone becomes a Christian?*

I understood that somehow, Jesus saved me from hell's eternal grasp—but who would save my car from being repossessed the next day?

I was a mess, misunderstanding grace. And worse, I didn't care. The Christian checklist was more important. Dress right and show up. Memorize the right Bible passages and recite to impress.

My faith was all about me.

As a card-carrying type A personality, my surrender didn't even register as a viable option. Surrendering was reserved for the goal-challenged weakling.

Instead of embracing freedom, I only grasped more rules. A relationship with a perfect God seemed incomprehensible to imperfect me. "You're drinking from the wellspring of life now," the Church People said.

What does that even mean?

I didn't know, but I knew I was on the fast track toward becoming one of those Christian hypocrites I loathed as a teenager and shunned as a young adult.

I cared only about decorating my façade, not about allowing God to change my heart. What people saw mattered. I was sure God understood my crusade to show His grace through my perfection.

He needed me, not the other way around.

It's a good thing God's divine patience and love embraces knuckleheads like me.

* * *

In retrospect, those early Christian years evoke feelings of stress and confusion. God's new life flowed in me, but I built spiritual dams against His hydration. I created a mental list of must-achieves before I felt worthy of partaking of His living water.

Get out of debt.

Control spending.

Lose weight.

Memorize all the right Bible passages.

Learn all the hymns.

And so on.

I remember vividly what it felt like to be that confused girl determined to save herself. All bravado on the outside, riddled with insecurity on the inside. The exhausted girl trying so hard to convince people she was worthy of their love.

Thirsty—but always drinking from my own well. My dusty cup.

What are you thirsty for?

Perhaps it's wealth, health, fame, a great name.

Each of us walks around with a certain level of dehydration. A thirst for something. And we've gotten used to it, chosen the threshold acceptable to us.

But why would we settle for that?

Becoming a Christian and new disciple of Jesus as an adult, I've experienced the difference between God's hydration and self-hydration. Living in the spiritual desert long enough eventually made me long for the Promised Land.

New disciples search for ways to quench thirsty souls that are parched by a dehydrated culture, shame, and guilt. Veteran disciples—that is, those who have walked that spiritual journey for many years—find themselves overcommitted, overcriticized, and shriveled dry from hectic demands.

God intends us to live differently.

Quenched: Christ's Living Water for a Thirsty Soul leads us to the depths of God's goodness and grace and shows us how we might drink from God's wellspring of life. Whether we are new disciples who are overwhelmed or exhausted longtime disciples, sometimes we lose the well's coordinates.

This book, divided into two parts, speaks with specificity to both new and veteran disciples. The first part focuses on those new to the faith and helps identify dehydrating behavior patterns. Relying on hard lessons learned from experience, I'll pinpoint biblical practices and spiritual disciplines aimed at breaking down the dams we build against God's wellspring of life.

The second part focuses on Christians who have walked the spiritual journey for many years. Perhaps you're worn down from decades of carefully crafting your façade as you slowly crumble on the inside. Spiritual warfare has taken its toll. We will work toward isolating and surrendering those dehydrating thought patterns and behaviors to turn back toward God's wellspring of life.

Wherever you are in your life, both sections of *Quenched* will offer you encouragement.

As you read, the most important truth to keep in mind is this: *the process isn't the solution.* This book uncovers how you can engage in the journey that ultimately reveals the solution(s) God has already prepared for you.

This is not a self-help book because Christianity isn't a twelve-step program to learn how to give up the world and quench our thirst. Jesus reveals that He is the living water that hydrates us from the soul out:

> Jesus said to her, "Everyone who drinks of this water will be thirsty again, but whoever drinks of the water that I will give him will never be thirsty again. The water that I will give him will become in him a spring of water welling up to eternal life." John 4:13–14

You may hesitate to dive in because you think you aren't ready. Well, I've never been ready to do anything God has called me to do. Some days, I still feel lost as a goose. But that's the point. We don't start the journey ready and filled, but seeking and thirsty. It is only in our thirst that we will be filled: "Blessed are those who . . . thirst for righteousness, for they shall be satisfied" (Matthew 5:6).

But please, embark on the journey, and know that you are not alone. Above all else, our Lord journeys with you: "I will never leave you nor forsake you" (Hebrews 13:5).

Perhaps you're experiencing a detour through a spiritual desert right now. Then keep reading. Keep walking. We all experience desert seasons.

Maybe you're in the middle of one of those seasons, or you have just emerged from one. Perhaps you see the dry, crackled ground ahead.

Are you ready to give up?

If that describes you, take heart. Jesus offers something better. He shows you the path to streams of living water that will quench your soul's thirst. He cannot bear watching you shrivel up without hope.

He throws you the ultimate lifeline.
His life is the line.
He doesn't care where you've been.
He doesn't care what you've done.
He cares about *you*.
And He's waiting at the well.

PART I

NEW DISCIPLES OF JESUS

"When the well is dry,
we know the worth of water."

Benjamin Franklin

CHAPTER 1

HYDRATION EXPLORATION

Jesus said to her, "Everyone who drinks of this water will be thirsty again, but whoever drinks of the water that I will give him will never be thirsty again. The water that I will give him will become in him a spring of water welling up to eternal life." ⁓John 4:13–14

The woman shuffled toward Jacob's well with lowered eyes. The noonday sun beat down in suffocating waves. The midday desert heat left her throat parched, but she didn't care. No one would be there at this hour.

She had planned it that way.

Water jug in hand, she traversed her usual path to the well outside of town, puffing up dust clouds in her wake. Head down. Just wanting to get there and back without incident.

The empty water container wasn't the only dry vessel she carried. Toting a heart and reputation battered by five marriages, she carried an empty soul as well. Her life, parched, dehydrated by worldly pursuits, was never quenched. Never satisfied.

Oh, she had heard it all. Hollow promises. Empty pledges. Still, she thirsted. Resigned, she knew she would return to the same unsatisfying well, time and time again—even knowing it would not, could not, satisfy the dryness of her soul.

Do you find yourself headed to the same well?

What do you seek as you shuffle forward through life? Do you plunge into the world, believing its treasures will quench your thirst, only to surface more thirsty than before?

Before I became a disciple of Jesus, that used to be me. Some days, it still is. The world's water always leaves us with dry souls and cracked hearts.

Here's how the story goes:

> So [Jesus] came to a town of Samaria called Sychar, near the field that Jacob had given to his son Joseph. Jacob's well was there; so Jesus, wearied as He was from His journey, was sitting beside the well. It was about the sixth hour. A woman from Samaria came to draw water. John 4:5–7

The Samaritan woman knew she wouldn't have to worry about a crowd of other women at the well. In that culture, drawing water was specifically designated as a female task (Genesis 24:11; Exodus 2:16). The women usually congregated there in the cool of the morning and evening. In those days, the water well served as a kind of coffeehouse or doughnut shop, like we would find in a small town today.

She could easily imagine the other women at the well. Could almost hear them chatting about their day, exchanging recipes and morsels of gossip. But by drawing water at the sixth hour—noon—she would avoid the peak of this activity at the well.

We know her history; we assume that the timing of her task reveals that the people shunned her. The other women—the insiders—would not have made her feel welcome. (If they had, she would have been at the well when they were.) Perhaps they gave her ugly looks or gossiped about her.

We, too, can show our disapproval of someone, make someone feel unwanted, without saying a word. Sometimes it even happens at church, "insiders" frowning at "outsiders." While we easily consign people to hell through silent judgment (or whether we ourselves have been consigned), that's not what Jesus does.

Do you sometimes feel like the Samaritan woman?

She had no idea that that day would be different. But meeting Jesus forever changed her life.

Chances are, you have experienced a life-changing day. Whether it looked like departing for college, getting married, having your first child, or laying to rest a beloved family member, days that change the trajectory are part of life.

But coming face-to-face with Jesus changes your eternity.

I experienced that truth in my early twenties. And it changed everything. Forever.

Since you're a new disciple of Jesus, I would venture a guess that receiving God's hydration invitation changed your life too. Did you experience uncertainty? Did you have fears? What did you struggle hardest to understand?

Here's how that life-changing day began to unfold for the Samaritan woman who, perhaps, believed life's surprises had run their course:

> Jesus said to her, "Give Me a drink." (For His disciples had gone away into the city to buy food.) John 4:7–8

At full midday sun when it was equator hot, the well was usually deserted. So who was the Man who sat there? Her steps slowed as she assessed the situation. One thing she understood was men. After five marriages, five divorces, and her current cohabitation with the next guy on the list, she knew what they wanted.

But something about this one seemed different. He wasn't a local. He was a Jew. Curiosity kept her moving toward the well. And in that moment, she crossed the line from curious bystander to intentional explorer.

The Truth About Explorers

Like you, like me, like every person whom God draws to Himself, we explore the reason why Love searches for someone like us.

The Samaritan woman notices that this Jewish stranger at the well addresses her with respect. No casting stones, innuendo, or assessing her from neck to navel.

Yet the long-standing hostility between Jews and Samaritans made her wary. Samaritans were despised by traditional Jews in those days. They were considered to be less-than. But look how Jesus changed that perception, as today, we often equate Samaritans with good deeds:

> Jesus replied, "A man was going down from Jerusalem to Jericho, and he fell among robbers, who stripped him and beat him and departed, leaving him half dead. . . . But a Samaritan, as he journeyed, came to where he was, and when he saw him, he had com-

passion. He went to him and bound up his wounds, pouring on oil and wine. Then he set him on his own animal and brought him to an inn and took care of him." Luke 10:30, 33–34

The Samaritan sounds like someone I want to have around when I'm facing trouble. Today, there are hospitals named after the good Samaritan. So why the bad rap in Jesus' day? Why did Jews hold such animosity toward Samaritans?

Samaria was another name for the Northern Kingdom, Israel. When the Assyrians conquered Israel, most of the Israelites were made slaves and taken away to Assyria or other conquered territories (2 Kings 17:6). This was standard Assyrian practice.

Concurrently, other conquered peoples, non-Jewish, were brought in to settle in the region of Samaria. As they lived together, the races became mixed, and a result was negativity (prejudice) toward Syria.

Judah, the Southern Kingdom, was conquered by Babylon. They did not follow the same practice as the Assyrians; hence the cleanliness of Judah (and other areas north of Samaria), and the uncleanness of the Samaritans.

By the first century, these new Samaritans embraced a mixture of cultural and religious influences, such as idol worship, child sacrifices, and other practices that the Jews highly opposed. Over time, traditional Jews went to great lengths to avoid associating with Samaritans. In fact, Jews often circumvented Samaria all together to prevent even coming in contact with Samaritans.

Divided into three distinct regions, each with its own ethnic and religious identity, the Holy Land stretched for one hundred twenty miles along the Mediterranean Sea. On the north side was Galilee and the south side was Judea. Samaria was in the middle. Although walking directly through Samaria took only two or three days, Jews would take up to six days to walk *around* it.

Jesus didn't need *to go through Samaria. He* chose *to.*

It is similar to our world today. There may be areas in cities that we hesitate to travel through, such as areas where increased violence, gangs, and illegal activity run rampant. There are countries that we don't visit and that airlines don't even fly over. We don't willingly put ourselves at risk by spending time in those places.

For the same reasons, Jews actively avoided Samaritans in that day, although their reasons included the desire to avoid contact with Samaritan differences in ethnic and moral standards, as well as safety.

For their part, Samaritans would harass any Jew traveling through their area just because they were Jewish. We can compare this to our modern-day racial profiling, when a person is harassed because of who he or she is, not because of what he or she has done.

That's the picture of the relationship between the Jews and Samaritans in Jesus' day. Knowing that cultural context helps us to better understand the initial exchange between Jesus and the Samaritan woman: "The Samaritan woman said to Him, 'How is it that you, a Jew, ask for a drink from me, a woman of Samaria?'" (John 4:9).

How many times have you exhibited similar behavior toward certain people or groups of people? Before becoming a Christian, I used to avoid Christians who openly professed their faith. Their confident talk about things I did not understand freaked me out. I had enough in my life freaking me out without adding another thing.

Explorers today don't fit a mold. They pop up at odd times and unusual places. Coffee shops, jury duty, anywhere but church—unless it's a wedding or funeral. Explorers are curious because they don't understand what Jesus has accomplished on their behalf. They've perhaps heard bits and pieces, so they're thirsty for truth.

Explorers tend to be adventurous, so they've usually sought meaning and contentment in many other wells. Career. Family. Making their mark. Leaving a legacy. But they have yet to find the legacy God has already prepared for them.

So they keep exploring.

Keep thirsting.

Explorers Realize They're Different

Explorers are driven by the search for worth, just like the Samaritan woman as she asks Jesus why He would even give her the time of day. She is aware that she is different. Acutely aware of her unworthiness.

She believes that her future in this life and the next is based on her worth as the person she is in that moment. But when we are born into the kingdom of God through Baptism, we become God's sons and daughters. Our value is based on that birth, not on what we are worth on our own.

As a daughter of the King, her future awaits—just as it does for you and me.

Explorers Ask Real Questions

The Samaritan woman, although she notices that Jesus is a Jew, doesn't sense hostility from Him. He simply requests a drink and reveals what He knows about her:

> The woman answered Him, "I have no husband." Jesus said to her, "You are right in saying, 'I have no husband'; for you have had five husbands, and the one you now have is not your husband. What you have said is true."
> John 4:17–18

She doesn't yet realize that Jesus is God in the flesh, although it is clear that somehow He knows her past and exactly what she's done. She notices He addresses her with polite respect. Men in those days—especially Jewish men—did not speak to women. Yet Jesus not only spoke to her, but His words were devoid of accusation and judgment.

What does that reveal about Jesus? That He cares more about reaching the lost with the hope of salvation than about observing cultural traditions that would protect His reputation. This was especially evident in His suffering and death. Jesus was God incarnate, but for her sake—for our sakes—the Lord of lords humbled Himself and became a beggar in need of a drink. Jesus' example shows us that when we are in need, we need not be ashamed to ask for help. Our greatest need is for Jesus' word of forgiveness and hope: we cannot dig our own well of salvation.

On those days when I realize that I have once again taken the willful plunge into sinful behavior, I wonder, *Jesus, how do You put up with me? How in the world can You be so patient and keep on loving me?* Once again, the truth of "birth, not worth" applies: When your child messes up, you don't throw her out with Thursday's garbage. We are His children. He never tosses us into a garbage can of hopelessness.

When I was a little girl, I remember hearing the phrase "God will get you for that." It caused me to fear God. Not a healthy, respectful fear, but fear of being struck by lightning. This remains a common perception in our culture, where many believe God sits on a cloud, lightning bolt in hand, waiting to smite us each time our pinky toe strays across some invisible boundary line.

That misconception caused me to shrink back from God rather than draw near. But our withdrawing from Him is never His intent; God wants us to draw near to Him. He thought of us before He laid the foundation of the world: "even as He chose us in Him before the foundation of the world, that we should be holy and blameless before Him. In love He predestined us for adoption as sons through Jesus Christ" (Ephesians 1:4–5).

Through God's great love, you and I have been adopted as His children. God's spoken authority formed creation, and His love—a trio of hearts—formed His children by molding, shaping, and drawing in close to exhale into us His breath of life.

Love changes everything, if we let it. By putting aside historical and cultural judgments, Jesus woos the woman to His wellspring of life with sincerity, kindness, and free-flowing love. He doesn't hold back to see if she can get her life together first. No, He extends grace.

To her.

To you.

To me.

Jesus' promise of grace flows like cool water over a dry, swollen tongue. His words give life to the parched desert traveler. And He invites you—He invites each of us—to drink deeply. He calls us out of our Sahara places to experience His monsoon of love.

Yet Jesus' simple request to the Samaritan woman goes far beyond quenching a physical thirst:

> If you knew the gift of God, and who it is
> that is saying to you, "Give Me a drink," you
> would have asked Him, and He would have
> given you living water. John 4:10

Many options could follow those three simple words "if you knew."

If you knew . . . peace.

If you knew . . . love.

If you knew . . . Me.

If you knew. *If you only knew.*

What words would you insert next? What weighs heavily on your heart and mind in this season of life?

If I only knew . . . my child would be born with a disability.

If I only knew . . . I would lose my job after moving into a new house.

If I only knew . . . my husband had a wandering eye before I said "I do."

If I only knew . . . my co-worker didn't know Jesus before she died.

If I only knew . . . my friend had one too many before climbing behind the wheel.

If can be a debilitating word, filled with regrets and second thoughts. But that's not how Jesus uses it. He offers that small word as hope for the future. He offers it to the Samaritan woman along with the living water of eternal life.

Love in a bucket.

A well that never runs dry.

Yet the Samaritan woman doesn't understand. She doesn't pick up on the spiritual undercurrent. She perceives only a logistical issue:

> Sir, You have nothing to draw water with, and the well is deep. John 4:11

The well was indeed deep. Archaeologists believe Jacob's well, where Jesus and the Samaritan woman met outside the city of Sychar, was the deepest well in Israel at that time. Significantly, *Sychar* meant "drunken," so named because of the drunkenness of its inhabitants. It provides some insight into the Samaritan woman's environment.

Jacob, one of Scripture's great patriarchs, purchased a piece of land and dug a well to provide for the needs of his family and livestock. The woman expresses her surprise that Jesus would claim to be greater than Israel's great patriarch, Jacob. She had been brainwashed by culture, but the truth remained: Jesus IS higher than any earthly patriarch.

Jacob's well intercepts an underground stream, so it receives constant refreshment. It has never been known to run dry and still flows fresh today.

Jesus' living water in us never runs dry either.

It's no coincidence that Jesus, the wellspring of life, chose to sit by the deepest well in the known world. The symbolism is stunning. Jesus had no way of reaching that physical water without help, and we have no way of reaching God's wellspring of life without Jesus.

Jesus is the Word made flesh. The Word sat next to Jacob's well in Samaria at that hour on that day. The woman had gone to the well in search of water.

Instead, the Source of living water sought her.

Explorers Need the Truth Spoken in Love

The Samaritan woman not only carried an empty water jug, she also carried a bad reputation.

Five prior husbands are a lot even by today's standards. In the first century, this was staggering. She is living in sin and she knows it, but she either cannot or chooses not to change anything.

You and I may look down on this woman and judge, yet we do not know why she had five husbands. Perhaps a few of them died unexpectedly. Or maybe a few of them had short tempers. In those days, a husband could divorce his wife merely by stating aloud three times, "I divorce you." She could have simply burned the toast for all we know.

We cannot judge her, because we *are her*. Whether in thought, word or deed:

> For all have sinned and fall short of the glory of God, and are justified by His grace as a gift, through the redemption that is in Christ Jesus. Romans 3:23–24

Jesus did not come to condemn us. He came to draw us to Him. We see His all-encompassing love extending to the woman at the well. He simply states the facts without judgment or harsh retribution. He desires to change her eternal trajectory:

> Jesus said to her, "Everyone who drinks of this water will be thirsty again, but whoever drinks of the water that I will give him will never be thirsty again. The water that I will give him will become in him a spring of water welling up to eternal life." John 4:13–14

I love the word "whoever" in that verse. God does not discriminate who should or should not receive His living water. He invites ALL.

The everyones.

The whoevers.

Throughout the New Testament, Jesus uses all-inclusive words like *"whoever* believes in Me" (John 6:35, emphasis added) and "if *anyone* thirsts" (John 7:37, emphasis added). Wonderful words of invitation that span the millennia.

Jesus didn't tell the Samaritan woman to get herself to church before He spoke to her. He met her on her territory. In the middle of her messy life.

Exactly where He meets you and me.

John 4:7 records Jesus' simple request for water from the Samaritan woman, and at the same time it provides several astounding contrasts: between God and man, between man and woman, between royalty and commonality, between wisdom and ignorance, between the unmarried and carelessly married, between purity and immorality, and between Jew and Gentile.

In the midst of those contrasts, Jesus and the Samaritan woman both want the same thing: *a drink of water.* The Samaritan woman had lived with an empty, parched soul her whole life. It's no wonder she sounds skeptical when Jesus makes the possibility of hydration so simple.

I felt uncertain when the Church People talked to me when I began going to church. I didn't feel worthy. I had trouble meeting their eyes.

Jesus' words strike at the very core of that heart issue. He tells the Samaritan woman, and me, and you, the game-changing news that the water He offers will not fill her jar.

It will fill her soul.

Explorers Come Thirsty

This living water that Jesus offers means flowing water. It is the same water referenced in the Old Testament:

> On that day living waters shall flow out from
> Jerusalem. Zechariah 14:8

Explorers expend energy; they need hydration. This flowing water referenced in Zechariah and offered by Jesus never stagnates because it's always moving.

The water that Jesus offers guarantees life, not life-robbing disease that resides in stagnant pools. His living water doesn't dry up in the heat of summer or when the heat is on in our lives.

When we do not rely on Jesus' living water to fill our longings, we try to fill that emptiness with other things. It may be any number of vices—or it may be alcohol, sex, food, work, or other things consumed to excess. It happens when we take the things that God intended for our pleasure and give them life-dehydrating power over our lives.

My whole adult life, this power has been food. When life got too scary and I needed immediate comfort, instead of turning to God, I turned to food. It still gets in the way today.

Jesus offers us the gift of His wellspring of life—we don't have to earn it, work for it, or even wrap it. He freely offers . . . but He will not force us to accept it.

Sometimes we get so caught up in our dehydrating sin that we don't recognize the life-threatening warning signs. I think the same was true for the Samaritan woman, who lived her life with one man after another. When she approaches the well that day, she assumes it was the familiar old well.

Another man.

Another proposition.

Same scenario.

Her soul-dehydrating numbness prevented her from recognizing that His well offered different results than the one she had been drawing from for far too long.

Jesus promises that all who receive His water of life will never be thirsty again. He goes far beyond the temporary satisfaction of ordinary water to the soul-altering, eternal hydration that only He offers. He promises that His living water will well up to eternal life, providing believers a glimpse into the life inhabited by the Holy Spirit.

Jesus' interaction with the Samaritan woman is the longest recorded conversation with one individual in all of Scripture. He offered her the opportunity to encounter Him in a real way when no one else was watching.

One on one.

Nothing to prove.

No one to impress or hide from.

And He meets us the same way: in shame-free transparent intimacy with Him. That safe place where we don't have to be fake or secretive to avoid looking stupid in front of friends.

In John 4:14, all three references to "water" (in Greek, *hydruo*) are the same word, so the type of water is not the compelling factor—it's who the water is connected to that makes the difference. For instance, taking baths does not mean that we get baptized each time we step into the tub. Only when the water is connected to the Word does it take on new meaning. Water becomes a spiritual catalyst when connected with Jesus, the Word made flesh.

In the original language, the word "I" is emphatically stressed in John 4:14: "whoever drinks of the water that *I* will give him will never be thirsty again" (emphasis added). Only water extended by and connected to Jesus, the Word, has the power to provide life beyond the grave. Jesus doesn't merely point out how to get to heaven; He IS the only way to heaven. He didn't descend to show us the way up; He made Himself the way to carry us there.

Explorers don't have to blaze a new trail or map out uncharted territory. The path is open to all who believe:

> Jesus said to him, "I am the way, and the truth, and the life. No one comes to the Father except through Me." John 14:6

From the Old Testament to the New Testament, God's promise remains consistent: When we thirst after Him, He faithfully quenches our spiritual thirst for all eternity. He is *the way*.

Explorers Understand Survival

The Samaritan woman strikes me as a survivor. Five husbands and living with a potential sixth may not sound like survival today, but let's give it some cultural context.

Women held no rights in biblical times. They were property to be exchanged or disposed of at the whim of husbands or fathers. Money, land, and property passed exclusively down the male line, with few exceptions. It was a gentleman's club of title and opportunity.

This woman survived by adapting to her surroundings and leveraging her resources. She believed her body and willingness were all she had, so that's what she deployed.

Then she met Jesus.

Perhaps yours is a similar story. Explorers tend to become experts at adapting to their surroundings. Adventures take explorers far and wide. Leveraging available resources means survival.

There are "three threes" when it comes to survival: we cannot survive three minutes without oxygen, three hours without shelter in extreme conditions, or three days without water. We all understand physical thirst. Our bodies require water to function; otherwise, our organs shut down.

Dehydration occurs when our bodies lose more fluid than we take in. We experience thirst when the pituitary gland secretes two hormones. One causes a physical reaction in the kidneys; the other causes the hypothalamus to send signals to the salivary glands to reduce secretions. Your body begins to hoard water as a form of self-preservation.

Physical thirst can be excruciating and dangerous. Dehydration can even lead to death. If you have ever been really, truly thirsty, then you have a sense of thirst in a spiritual sense.

Not everyone recognizes spiritual thirst. In our instant-gratification culture, we become confused about what truly satisfies. Today, we have many shallow wells to choose from to try to satiate physical thirst. What do you thirst after in this season of your life?

Stability, financial or otherwise?

Job security?

Close family ties?

How does drawing from these wells quench your thirst?

One of the most startling symptoms of severe dehydration is that we do not produce tears when we cry. It's the same with spiritual dehydration: our soul is so dry that we cannot shed tears over our sin, much less the sin of others.

An important factor to consider is that drinking is a voluntary action. Like the proverbial horse at the trough, you cannot make someone drink.

As Christians, our job is not to make people drink from the well. Our job is to point people to the Fountain of Living Water. God Himself will draw the people. We are simply a directional sign pointing to the One who enables ALL things.

Three important, consecutive words appear twice in John 4:14: "*I will give*" (emphasis added). Those three words compose this wonderful promise of hope. There is no ambiguity in those words. They provide a clear concise promise from Jesus: *I will give*.

This incredible promise of God is a *gift*. We don't have to buy it, earn it, or prove ourselves worthy to receive it. Jesus gives it wholeheartedly to *all* who thirst after Him.

Explorers Get the Word Out

After hearing Jesus' stunning words, the Samaritan woman cannot contain herself. She goes back to the town to invite the people:

> "Come, see a man who told me all that I ever did. Can this be the Christ?" They went out of the town and were coming to Him. John 4:29–30

She did not run to them for protection from a stalker who knew all about her life. She needed to tell them about Jesus and His life-giving promise. She was so excited, she didn't think about herself. Her past. Her reputation. What the people thought of her.

The message took priority.

And the townspeople who heard her story about Jesus saw the genuineness of her words. They saw past her past. They saw only the One she was pointing them toward.

That's our job as Christians. As a new Christian, it may be uncomfortable. But when God reveals His message to you, you will not be able to keep silent about it. You, like me, will want to tell those who are dying of thirst about the Thirst Quencher who changes their destiny.

Can we, like Christ, look past people's past? Or are we more interested in focusing on their faults instead of telling them about the Fountain of Life?

Jesus focuses on our future. He pays attention to our path, not our past.

The Samaritan woman stumbled through the desert, looking for water. And the Water of Life found her instead.

In her excitement to tell others about the One who quenched her thirst, she left her water jar at the well. She had sought to fill a physical jar. She received a spiritual ocean instead.

C. S. Lewis captured this seeking experience:

> If we find ourselves with a desire that nothing in this world can satisfy, the most probable explanation is that we were made for another world. [1]

And because of her witness to the town, many more believed, as well:

> Many Samaritans from that town believed in Him because of the woman's testimony, "He told me all that I ever did." So when the Samaritans came to Him, they asked Him to say with them, and He stayed there two days. And many more believed because of His word. They said to the woman, "It is no longer because of what you said that we believe, for we have heard for ourselves, and we know that this is indeed the Savior of the world." John 4:39–42

Her excitement about the wonders revealed to her turned her into a walking advertisement for Jesus. When we're excited and pumped about something, we turn into walking marketing campaigns. When I return from a fascinating place, I can't stop talking about the places I explored and experienced.

The Samaritan woman was spreading the news about what Jesus promised. And all the attention went straight to Him.

With God's Holy Spirit inside every believer, we become spotlights shining His light wherever we go. When we shine the spotlight on ourselves, it blinds us to truth. Makes us see spots in others.

Our job is to point the spotlight on Jesus and get out of the way.

How Explorers Move to the Next Stage

Exploring is a much-needed endeavor. Yet at some point, explorers, filled by the hydrating love and grace of God, need to actively engage in that love relationship. The Samaritan woman exhibited that truth when she left her jar at the well, indicating her willingness for God to fill her.

Bible Class

Today, this would look like our committing to regular Bible class and worship. Learning and allowing our knowledge of God to grow is an indispensable step on our Christian journey.

Prayer

It also looks like spending regular time in prayer. At first, in my experience, that proved a daunting task. I mean, what was I supposed to say to God—to the One who created me and everything I see in nature? This got easier for me when a wonderful Christian lady advised that prayer just looks like a conversation with your best friend. Conversations where we talk, and also spend time listening.

Embracing Christian Friendships

Actively seeking out Christian friends is important. The people you surround yourself with have great influence in your life. Choose wisely.

The bottom line? You may be new to Christianity, but you are not new to God. He planned out every day of your life before the foundation of the world:

> [God], who saved us and called us to a holy
> calling, not because of our works but because
> of His own purpose and grace, which He gave

us in Christ Jesus before the ages began.
2 Timothy 1:9

He has pursued you all your life and has intentionally sought a relationship with you, just like He had with Adam and Eve in the Garden of Eden.

Being a follower of Christ isn't about religion or a denomination or a particular church. It never will be. It's about relationship—God reaching for man. Reaching for us, who have fallen when words and actions have scraped our heart raw. Reaching for us even when we try to hide pain with perfectionism; even when we feel like what we've done is beyond redemption.

God will continue to pursue us. He asks us the same question that He asked Adam and Eve: "Where are you?" We attempt to hide our sin from God, just as they did. Even when we try to shove our sins under the bed, He knows our exact coordinates. Exactly which dark pile of sin we're hiding in the shadows of shame and guilt.

God continuously invites us to step into His light of redemption. He never stops wooing us into a vibrant relationship with Him. He knows that the alternative means death. So He releases His aquifer of love to hydrate us from the inside out.

Always flowing fresh.

Never running dry.

A PAUSE AT THE WELL

Let's take a moment to pause for some practical application. First, we need to take time to clearly identify a few important things:

1. As a new Christian, list the top five things you struggle with most. (For instance, I struggled with completely trusting Someone I couldn't see.)

2. What are some of your current habits or behaviors that seem to deplete your energy, wear you out emotionally, or interfere with spending time with God in prayer and studying His Word?

3. What activities energize or delight you? (For instance, I love photography because it allows me to marvel at God's magnificent creation.)

I realize that many people would rather be anywhere else than clocking in at a 9-to-5 job, but unless you're a trust-fund baby or independently wealthy, that's simply a part of life. But take a moment to compare your answers to questions 2 and 3. Which list most identifies how you spend a typical day?

If you find your life stuck in the list in question 2, it's time to make some adjustments. Attitude plays a large part in how we handle our day-to-day activities.

You may not like spending most of your day at your job, but it doesn't have to deplete you. I work at a law firm from 8:30 a.m. until 5:00 p.m., Monday through Friday. I could choose to see this work as a waste of time. I could choose to grumble and mumble about not spending my days with my nose buried in Scripture or writing new Bible studies.

However, I am exposed to people in that environment that I would miss if I were sitting at home. From brilliant lawyers with analytical minds to corporate executives of Fortune 500 companies, the privilege of interacting with them keeps me sharp and on my toes. It's also a school for human behavior and for observing how the world operates on a global scale. How would I learn to reach professionals with the Gospel if I don't understand how corporate America operates?

Attitude matters, and keeping your eyes on Jesus makes the difference.

* *

PRAYER STARTER

*After studying this chapter, take some time to pray.
Ask God to reveal what areas of your life you need
to surrender to His hydration.*

* *

CHAPTER 2

ENOUGH WITH THE EXCUSES ALREADY

Now there is in Jerusalem by the Sheep Gate
a pool, in Aramaic called Bethesda, which has
five roofed colonnades. In these lay a multi-
tude of invalids—blind, lame, and paralyzed.

~John 5:2–3

The stifling desert heat made breathing difficult for those who gathered here. The unpleasant odor of stagnant water filled their nostrils. Beautiful colonnades surrounded the pool where the people lounged, but the people did not notice.

Desperation was slowly suffocating them.

For thirty-eight years, the man had tried to reach the pool's edge, but his body wouldn't cooperate. We don't know his name, only that he bore the label "invalid." He lived on a mat near a pool called Bethesda in first-century Jerusalem. He called this place home because he believed this water could heal him.

There he sat, day after day, waiting. Languishing. Swatting flies. Here's how the story goes:

> Now there is in Jerusalem by the Sheep Gate a pool, in Aramaic called Bethesda, which has five roofed colonnades. In these lay a multitude of invalids—blind, lame, and paralyzed. One man was there who had been an invalid for thirty-eight years. When Jesus saw him lying there and knew that he had already been there a long time, He said to him, "Do you want to be healed?" John 5:2–6

Some may perceive this question as taunting or even cruel. Perhaps, as a new disciple, you believe He's asked you that type of question: "Your life is falling apart; don't you know how much you need Me?"

Jesus never asks a question without already knowing the answer. He knows some people don't want to get better. Some prefer whining, complaining, and expecting handouts to hard work. Perhaps that was the case for the man near the pool at Bethesda.

But really, if you have lived disabled for thirty-eight years, what kind of question is that? Wouldn't you want to get well?

The Excuses Game

At one time or another, we've all tried to convince ourselves that we're fine. That everything is running like clockwork. But this is an illusion.

When I first started attending church, I convinced myself that the Church People needed me. They needed a *real* perspective on life. Not the vanilla world inside church, where everyone is content in his or her safe Christian bubble.

But that invalid was me, excusing away my mess of a life. I needed Jesus desperately, but I chose not to see it. After all, admitting my weaknesses to strangers and to Someone I can't see was not in my playing cards. They would make me feel stupid. Hurl stones of judgment. Cast knowing looks of pity.

Thanks, but no thanks.

But the truth is, once I honestly assessed my falling-apart life, I ran out of excuses. Besides, coming up with excuse after excuse was exhausting.

So, two years into attending church, when my boyfriend proposed, I had to make some serious decisions. Saying yes to him meant saying yes to the Church People.

And saying no to any more excuses. Excuses for not engaging in a relationship with Christ. Excuses for why I couldn't control my spending habits. Excuses for so many things.

Offering excuses keeps us trapped in the past, old habits, and unhealthy thought patterns. But more important, when we choose excuses, we willfully keep Jesus at arm's length. And if there's one thing I've learned over the past twenty-three years of walking with Him, the last place we want Jesus is at arm's length.

Let's look at some excuses that the man near the pool of Bethesda could have offered. They ring true for me. And I bet you'll find that you have used some of these excuses as well.

Excuse #1: "I Don't Need to Be Healed, Thank You Very Much."

In first-century Jerusalem, it wasn't the custom to help those who had serious physical ailments. People stricken with a disability weren't considered to have a medical issue; they were considered to have a sin issue (John 9:1–2).

In those days, people looked down their noses at the sick because they believed that anyone who suffered illnesses had done something wrong. Perhaps the person had stolen, lied, or failed to offer a proper sacrifice to God. Maybe his parents had done something wrong, so God was punishing him instead.

The religious leaders of the day suggested repentance as the only way to get well. To some extent, we still subscribe to that thinking.

In this Bible passage, the invalid (like all those gathered around the pool) believed that an angel of the Lord descended to stir the pool at Bethesda (John 5:7, footnote). We don't know how often this stirring took place. It could have been every day, once a week, or once every six months. But the people who gathered there believed that whoever was the first to touch the freshly stirred water would be cured of disease or healed of disability.

There are places in the world today that purport to have some sort of therapeutic water as well. Many people travel to these mineral baths and hot springs, and underlying their journey nestles the hope of healing.

To function just like everybody else.

To be normal again.

To be accepted.

But how many of us like to admit that we need healing of anything? It makes us think we're weak, and we don't like to be called weak—or to be perceived as such.

That leaves us vulnerable.

I remember firsthand the great lengths I went to as a new disciple to appear rock solid. Like I had all my stuff together, even though my excuses were hollowing out my insides with shame and guilt. I should've dived headfirst into God's wellspring of life. But maintaining appearances seemed more important at the time.

The man at the Bethesda pool faced a very real problem. To have the chance at healing, he believed he had to be the first to touch the water after it had been stirred. However, invalids don't break speed records. And since those who gathered there held the same belief, multitudes lounged around the fringe of the pool, waiting for their chance.

Picture the scene in your mind's eye. The water stirs. The lame and paralyzed notice. The buzz of excitement alerts the blind. And the race to the water's edge begins. Pushing. Shoving. Intent looks on desperate faces.

The odds of this man reaching the water first were slim to none, so he waited. For thirty-eight years he waited. He waited longer by that pool than the life expectancy of some people of his day.

If you were an invalid and believed the water could heal you, how long would you live on a mat?

This man's mat was literally a mat, but it embodies other issues.

For you and me, that mat could represent any number of strongholds. A stronghold is any argument or pretension that sets itself up against the knowledge of God (2 Corinthians 10:5). In other words, anything we hold in higher esteem than God's Word is a stronghold.

An argument is a philosophy, reasoning, or scheme of the world. And this represents a huge issue for new disciples because culture tends to be our plumb line. Culture influences our life on every level, including our personal assessment; it guides what we hold important, and it develops our worldview. Breaking or changing those arguments takes relentless prayer and dedicated time studying God's Word. We cannot know God's reasonings and guidelines for living if we don't practice these disciplines.

Pretensions have to do with anything man-centered. Things such as pride and entitlement (to name two) present significant roadblocks against surrendering our thoughts, hearts, and paths to God for holy refinement.

The man near the pool at Bethesda could have easily used a physical ailment as his excuse, yet it would have covered many other issues, as we'll discover. Instead, he lived on his mat. For thirty-eight years. A staggering amount of time.

Most of us wouldn't have that much patience. As a Type A personality, I like to believe I would have been a little more proactive about achieving my goal. I would have called in my posse. You know, my trusted friends who would work crowd control and would carry me to the water and sit me down, right on the edge.

Or would I?

Would you?

Excuse #2: "I've Got Friends; Who Needs Jesus?"

Think of your circle of friends. Those you do life with.

You go to church with them, enjoy dinner and a movie, and share struggles and dreams.

This man's friends were most likely those surrounding him. The same is true for many of us. Our closest friends, those cherished ones who help us in times of need, oftentimes live close by.

This man's close-proximity friends were the lame, blind, and paralyzed. They couldn't get to the water themselves, so how could they help him? And would they even want to if it prevented them from reaching it first?

Looking from the outside in, it may be easy to judge this man, but this story stops me short every time I read it. Although my goals are not the same as his, I have struggled to reach them too.

I'm sure each of us has.

A healthier lifestyle. Financial freedom. Relational bliss. Meaningful friendships. If you're like me, you don't break Olympic records going after these lofty goals. I'll do it tomorrow. Or the next day. Like Scarlett O'Hara, we'll "think about that tomorrow."

We stay thirsty.

We keep searching.

We may have many friends, but we really *do* need Jesus.

As I was growing up, every so often I heard two names: God and Jesus. Whether it was from how people said the names or from a stirring deep within me, I couldn't tell, but from my sporadic church attendance, I understood that God was the "Big Guy." Creator of everything. But Jesus? I had no clue. He was called the Son, but I didn't remember hearing that God was married. Jesus was part of the Trinity—whatever that was.

How could I be so ignorant of what so many others seemed to know?

Did you feel that way?

Although Mom and Dad were both raised going to church, it wasn't a regular part of my childhood. Dad worked in real estate, so his weekends were spent touring clients, showing houses, and writing contracts. Church was not a priority for him. Consequently, it was not a priority for me.

There was something about those names, though. I had so many questions, but I didn't rush to find answers. I was blind, but I didn't know it. Parched, but I couldn't feel it.

Looking back, I see that I was no different from the invalid by the pool. I was dehydrated from the inside out, but chose to ignore it. Life was comfortable.

No need to shake things up.

I liked my mat where it sat, right in the middle of my friends.

Perhaps you do too.

I had a loving family and plenty of friends. Friends represent an integral part of our lives. They exercise a great deal of influence over the decisions we make.

Friends provide a sense of belonging, so it goes without saying that you go with the flow to retain that privilege.

47

But what if your friends have harmful habits?

I live near Houston, the fourth-largest city in the United States. Gangs are rampant in every culture and race. Without exception, gangs are extremely violent. They have to be in order to maintain control of their territories. In many instances, initiation for acceptance into a gang requires a person to prove loyalty by committing a crime ranging from burglary to murder.

Now, I realize that probably doesn't represent you or your group of friends. But pause for a moment and think. When you're around your inner circle of friends, do you sometimes go along with what they want just so you don't cause waves?

For several months during my early twenties, I connected into a circle of friends who liked the big-city clubbing scene. To fit in and be accepted, I went along. And to be brutally honest, I'm surprised I'm still alive. Literally. We'll visit that more in a later chapter.

Good choices in life are easier to make, maintain, and nurture when your circle of friends is moving in the same upward direction. If they don't understand your newfound faith, taking time to explain it to them is important.

But take note of how they react.

If they ridicule you or question your sanity, those people are not the ones who are willing to support your friendship, let alone your new faith journey. It may be time to rethink how much time you spend with them. I had to make those same decisions. They are hard, gut-wrenching choices.

But they are absolutely necessary.

Excuse #3: "It's Too Hard to Change My Whole Lifestyle."

Sometimes we adopt certain lifestyles because we're too lazy to change or don't care enough to change. Making lifestyle changes requires commitment, discipline, and a dedicated support group.

Or, again, we can choose to make excuses.

Excuses blocked my path to the water, just like the invalid in our Bible story. We see his excuses as the story continues:

> The sick man answered Him, "Sir, I have no one to put me into the pool when the water is stirred up, and while I am going another steps down before me." John 5:7

I don't know about you, but I find it hard to believe that after thirty-eight years, he couldn't move closer to the pool. Even if he dragged himself two inches each day, he would've eventually made enough progress to reach that water. When the mass of people rushed to the pool's edge each time it was stirred, there must have been some space between them so he could move a little closer.

But he was so busy making excuses, he wasn't really understanding Jesus' question: *"Do you want to be healed?"* Jesus wasn't asking him why he couldn't walk. Jesus was asking a deeper question. But the man's mind was too preoccupied with thinking up excuses to hear Jesus' real question.

The man had no idea who was asking him the question—no idea that Jesus had the divine power to change his circumstance.

He just made more excuses.

Sometimes we default to excuses because it's easier than honest self-examination. Admitting we harbor jealousy, judgment, anger, hatred, or any number of ugly emotions proves painful. Acknowledging the sins we cling to makes it hard at look ourselves in the mirror.

So we, like the man by the pool, make excuses.

Perhaps he just wanted to fit in somewhere. Feel accepted. Maybe he didn't want to ruffle feathers, have his motives questioned, or be accused of putting himself in front of others.

So there he languished.

The water so close, yet unreachable.

The man never identified himself as an invalid. He said only that he needed help to reach the pool. Scripture tells us only that others had labeled him.

We often do the same.

Only a syllabic stress alters the meaning of the word *invalid*.

INvalid means you are disabled.

In**VAL**id means you are inconsequential.

In society's eyes, this man was both.

In Jesus' eyes, he was neither.

Excuse #4: "But, I Can't . . ."

Excuses impaired the behavior of the man near the pool at Bethesda. Instead of answering Jesus' question directly, he offered excuses for his behavior, beginning with, "I have no one" and "while I am going."

In other words: *"I can't."* Few excuses cause lame behavior more effectively than those two debilitating words.

The original Greek of John 5:3 refers to *lame* (or *invalid*) as being deprived of a foot or being maimed. Blindness can be hidden. But the maimed cannot hide. Whether caused by a wound to the body, heart, soul, or mind, behavior of the maimed is visible.

The man near the pool was physically disabled. But I suggest that his physical condition eventually became his *state of mind*.

In the greater scheme of life, wars are often won or lost in our minds before they ever occur in real time.

For instance, have you ever met an angry, bitter person? I believe we all have. Don't you wonder what happened to that person that resulted in such an attitude? Chances are, he or she suffered a relational break or difficulty. His or her heart was wounded by unforgiveness, and if that hurt is never worked through properly, unforgiveness becomes a *state of mind*.

Whether it's refusing to forgive an ex-spouse, ex-boss, or wayward child, holding grudges causes us to limp from the inside out.

People who don't forgive set their mind to hold on to the hurt and nurse bitterness. Our mind-set, or attitude, plays a vital role in how we choose to behave. Believing "I can't" forfeits the race before we even reach the start line.

There is an incredible group of kids who learn tae kwon do in my church's community center. In fact, they have become so good that they have won several championships, both as a team and as individuals. Normally, that wouldn't be extraordinary. However, these kids are disabled and physically challenged. I'll bet their vocabulary doesn't contain the phrase "I can't." Their positive attitude, phenomenal instructors, and amazing support group make all the difference. It never occurs to them to offer excuses to avoid participation.

I've offered plenty of "I can't" excuses in my lifetime—to parents, siblings, employers, volunteer recruiters, you name it. But each time, I felt lame afterward. Maimed by laziness, bad choices, and self-centeredness.

If you struggle with defaulting to the "I can't" excuse, let me point you to one particular Bible verse that God used to change my attitude:

> I can do all things through Him who strengthens me. Philippians 4:13

As a new disciple, I plastered that verse everywhere. I taped it to my car's dashboard, wrote on the top of my calendar, tabbed and highlighted it in my Bible. That daily visual reminder of God's presence in me gave me courage to stop making excuses and start allowing God access to begin dismantling those harmful, spiritual dams I had built.

Ironically, Philippians 4:13 was one of the Bible verses I memorized in the beginning of my faith journey when I was trying to just blend in. But the Lord chose to bury those words in the soil of my heart until they took root. And although I didn't realize it at the

51

time, that verse became instrumental in surrendering my "I can't" attitude so that I could understand that "Jesus can."

Regardless of our inabilities, God is able.

I am so thankful that Jesus didn't offer excuses on Good Friday.

We would have been maimed for all eternity.

Excuse #5: "I Won't Blindly Trust Someone I Can't See."

One of the greatest challenges I faced as a new disciple was the fact that I can't physically see the One I was following. "Blind faith," as some call it. For me it appeared to be an Olympic hurdle.

The Gospel of John mentions the blind as it identifies the groups hanging out by the pool at Bethesda.

> In these lay a multitude of invalids—blind, lame, and paralyzed. John 5:3

Since I've worn corrective lenses for almost twenty-five years, I automatically associate blindness with the lack of physical sight. I'm nearsighted, so farther means fuzzier.

As I studied John 5:3, I thought about two other areas of life where we struggle with blindness: relational blindness and spiritual blindness.

When it comes to relational blindness, we come to an area where farther means fuzzier. Understanding another person's desires, expectations, needs, and motives takes monumental time, tenacity, and relentless prayer. If you are (or have been) married, then you fully realize the investment of time marriage requires. Yet even when we invest a lot of time, relational storms can still blind us. We get caught in a funnel cloud of hurt and drama that whirls around our marriage until sometimes we can't even see our hand in front of our face. And when that happens, we may become spiritually blind. Our emotions easily drown out God with questions like:

How am I supposed to focus on God with all this going on?

Did God cause this storm in the first place? What does He expect me to do about it?

What did I do to deserve this?

Why do those who hate or ignore God seem to have seamless, smooth lives?

When I endured the storm of an unexpected divorce, I asked so many spiritually blind questions. And even worse, I supplied my own self-deprecating answers:

How could I have missed the signs? You are so stupid!

Was I simply too preoccupied with myself? Me? Selfish?

Didn't I do everything I knew to be a good wife? Obviously not; look what happened.

How can I ever trust someone to that degree again? You can't. They're all the same.

Not very uplifting self-talk in front of the mirror. On the other side of that painful storm, the errors in my questions glared back. They all included "I" as the sole cause or problem.

I had fallen into that same trap of those blind first-century people who assumed the invalid had done something wrong to deserve what he got. It took a solid year of Christian counseling to remove my spiritual blindness.

As a new disciple, perhaps you struggle like I did with spiritual blindness when it comes to fully trusting God. Perhaps you have questions like:

How can I form any kind of bond with someone whose eyes I cannot look into?

How am I supposed to entrust my life into hands I cannot see?

Isn't God just going to do what He wants anyway, regardless of what I decide?

Our circumstances may blind us, but God remains close. Although we can't see Him, everything He created points us to Him:

> For since the creation of the world God's
> invisible qualities—His eternal power and
> divine nature—have been clearly seen, being
> understood from what has been made, so that
> people are without excuse. Romans 1:20 (NIV)

When you and I behold God's magnificent creation, the precision of its order, and the intelligent design so clearly evident, it provides hope. Out of all His creation, human beings are the only creatures He made with a soul. In that special place, God pours in His Holy Spirit, enabling us to be in relationship with Him.

As long as we are not blind to God, no storm can overtake us.

But sometimes our blindness correlates directly to our culture. Each day, we enter the rat race to check things off on our impressive to-do lists. Chief of sinners though I am! This one knocks me upside the head more often than any other. That pressure to keep up.

Stay relevant.

Prove myself valuable.

For example, I recently drove into my driveway after work and noticed a "For Sale" sign in my next-door neighbor's yard. They had not mentioned they were considering a move, so I called them. Their jaw-dropping response? He and his family had moved out a month ago. I had not even noticed they were gone. Ugh. Talk about a wake-up call.

Spiritual blindness also creates significant damage in our lives. We become blind to the blessings that God surrounds us with each and every day. Blind to the nudging of the Holy Spirit to go down a different path. Blind to the power of the cross.

People in biblical times struggled with spiritual blindness, as well:

Judas betrayed.

David spied.

Peter denied.

When we put our own desires and needs above God's, we can expect that a storm is around the corner.

I chose to believe that I needed the finer things in life to gain respect. All I gained was mountainous debt and stress headaches from the intense pressure to keep up with the Joneses. As long as I tried to make myself valuable, I denied the worth of Jesus' sacrifice that renders me priceless.

There are so many obstacles that blind us. The race God put before us is hard enough. I don't want to run it without my sights set on Him.

I bet you don't either.

Excuse #6: "Being Christian Isn't Popular."

As a new disciple, I longed for the Church People's approval, so inside the church's walls, I claimed to be a Christian. But outside those walls?

Well, this excuse was a huge stumbling block in my journey. I wasn't fully comfortable yet with following Someone I couldn't see. So how could I explain this new faith journey without sounding like I'd lost my marbles?

How others perceive us often paralyzes us from stepping out and following our calling.

There's a lot more to paralysis than the physical.

The final group at the pool of Bethesda intrigues me most: the paralyzed. Although some were certainly physically paralyzed, I suggest that many at the pool were subject to some other form of paralysis, just as you and I can be too.

For example, we can be paralyzed by fear. Frozen by doubt. Immobilized by the need for unilateral acceptance. And the list goes on.

Since I longed for people's approval, I was paralyzed by their perception of me. Being a Christian wasn't cool in my nonchurch circles, so I distanced myself from talking to and acting like one.

Paralysis leaves us parched beyond other disabilities because nonphysical paralysis begins in our minds. That's where the real battle originates. Our minds can play nasty tricks on us.

I'm the biggest chicken on the planet when it comes to scary movies. Even if I see only a sixty-second commercial, I start hearing creaking doors and seeing shadows dart past out of the corner of my eye.

I know—ridiculous, right?

They are just figments (or, as my friend Susan says, "fig newtons") of an overactive imagination. There really wasn't a bloodsucking monster with hairy feet and one big eyeball waiting around the corner. My fears and perceptions weren't real, but the longer I dwelt on them, the more fangs I gave them.

Sometimes we willingly choose paralysis in order to control our surroundings. To stay safe, if you will.

Leaders often struggle with paralysis when it comes to risk taking, especially in the Church. They fear failure or harsh words hurled by those who disagree with decisions made, so they compromise or suffer in frustrated paralysis. And so another unfulfilled leader limps along.

Which category are you in during this season of life? Are you lame, blind, or paralyzed? Perhaps you suffer a tad from all three.

If that's the case, the invalid next to the pool at Bethesda provides an important insight: despite all of his excuses, his soul craved and longed after a hope he could not shake.

A better life.

Perhaps earning an honest day's wages.

Something.

King David captures this longing of our soul:

> As a deer pants for flowing streams, so pants my soul for You, O God. My soul thirsts for God, for the living God. Psalm 42:1–2

Those verses reveal a soul thirsty for something greater than the stirring water offered to the blind, lame, and paralyzed at the pool at Bethesda. The words reveal a longing for water that hydrates our very soul.

Streams of living water that heal far more than flesh and bone.

Sometimes we believe we need physical healing, but sometimes that's a symptom of something greater. Our Savior sees our deeper need.

For thirty-eight years, the invalid wanted to approach the place of healing water. In the end, the Source of living water came to him. Just like He came to the woman at the well.

And the invalid was never the same again.

> Jesus said to him, "Get up, take up your bed, and walk." And at once the man was healed, and he took up his bed and walked. John 5:8–9

As long as we offer excuses not to engage in God's bigger plan for our lives, we merely stick our pinky toe in God's wellspring.

As long as we're more devoted to remaining on our safe mat than surrendering our lives to Jesus, we'll be stuck in our wounded self.

As long as blending into the crowd is more important than standing for Christ, we'll be stuck in emptiness.

As long as retaining control over our life takes precedence over surrendering our paralysis to Him, our mat will stay rooted in ineffectiveness.

Surrendering our dehydrating excuses to receive God's hydration allows His wellspring of love to fill us to overflowing.

In that surrender, God transforms our excuses into confidence in Christ, clearing the way for Him to remove those life-sucking excuses to which we cling.

It starts with hearing His call, receiving His calling, and surrendering our individual will to God's will.

His good, pleasing, and perfect will.

A PAUSE AT THE WELL

Let's take a moment to pause for some practical application. Excuses prevent us from surrendering our whole lives to God and growing in faith.

1. Although there may be more than one, which excuse best describes this season of your faith journey?

2. What is that excuse trying to mask from God and others?

3. If fear is behind that excuse, what are you afraid of?

Searching Scripture for God's hope-filled promises works toward dissipating our fear and uncertainty. Take a moment to say Philippians 4:13 aloud: "I can do all things through Him who strengthens me." Now take some time to write that verse in several places where you can see it several times a day.

Relying on God's strength will turn your excuses into a heart willing to serve Him wherever He calls you. You may still deal with fear, but knowing that He goes before you steadies your knees to walk down that path, confident that He will guide you every step of the way.

· ·

PRAYER STARTER

Take some time to ask God to identify the areas of
your life where offering excuses comes by default.
One by one, surrender them to God, and ask
Him to strengthen you against fear.

· ·

CHAPTER 3

JESUS KNEW HOW TO PARTY

On the last day of the feast, the great day, Jesus stood up and cried out, "If anyone thirsts, let him come to Me and drink. Whoever believes in Me, as the Scripture has said, 'Out of his heart will flow rivers of living water.'" ~John 7:37–38

The pulsating music, flashing strobe lights, and gyrating bodies created a surreal scene. Intent faces formed a stag line around the dance floor's circumference, eyes scanning potential dance partners like hungry lions at a kill. Prowling. Desperate.

It was party time.

Every Friday night for six months, this scene was part of my life when I was twenty-two. New friends that I met at work loved the clubbing scene. So into the Houston nightlife I dived headfirst.

Smoky dance floors, exotic drinks, and men who knew how to dance and say a good line mesmerized my warped Cinderella mentality. This new experience made me realize what a sheltered life I had lived. I was fascinated by the glitter, cowboy hats, tight blue jeans, and atmosphere.

I jumped into that lifestyle with both feet and a smile on my face. After all, wasn't this what young women living in a big city did to find a potential mate? All I had to do was make myself available to all the world had to offer, right?

I learned how to two-step, twirl, and line-dance with the best of them. I didn't like the taste of beer, so I usually sipped on one mixed drink the whole night, earning me the designated driver position.

I thought I was having the best time of my life.

Until one night changed everything.

One evening, after spending three hours at one particular club, the friend who drove us there decided to go home with the man she had danced with all night. However, she never told me she took the car. So at 2:00 a.m., when the club closed, I found myself standing in the parking lot with no ride and no money for a cab. The man I had been dancing with most of the evening saw my predicament and offered to take me to his place to wait until my friend came to get me. I didn't see another alternative, so I accepted.

Calling my parents was not an option. They didn't know about this new aspect of my life, and I certainly had been raised to behave better than I was acting that night. The only smart thing I did the whole evening was to insist on driving since he was in no condition to get us anywhere safely.

How in the world did I get myself into such a quandary?

If you've ever backed yourself into a dangerous corner, you know what I mean. Did you try to assign the blame to anything and everyone else? Believe me, I tried to do that, but there was nowhere to lay it except at my own doorstep.

Blame never changes our foolish choices; and change doesn't happen unless we're forced to look in the mirror. Hard conversations there can alter our decisions, attitude, and direction.

We arrived at his apartment, and I helped him inside. He said he would pour us a drink, but first we could get comfortable on the couch together.

Gulp.

By the sheer grace and mercy of God, he passed out as soon as he hit the sofa. There I stood. Taking in that scene.

It was 3:00 a.m. I was standing in a strange man's apartment. In an unfamiliar part of town. With no money and no way to leave.

Talk about a wake-up call.

Survival instincts finally kicked in. I noticed a large jar of change next to his telephone, so I fished out enough to pay for a cab and got out of there as fast as I could. I never saw him again.

That evening could've turned out much worse than it did. I understood that I'd been given a second chance to make some important lifestyle changes.

Keeping an eye on the scary-looking cab driver in that filthy cab as I headed back to my apartment, I had ample time to think. To beat myself up for being so stupid. I usually exhibited more common sense.

That night was my last in the Houston clubbing scene. I started making some necessary lifestyle changes, beginning with my circle of friends. They certainly hadn't forced me to do anything; the gullibility and stupidity were all mine.

Friends have great influence in our lives because we some-times act differently when they're around. Act braver than we are. Agree to escapades we normally wouldn't participate in.

If you ever saw the movie *Grease*, you saw that truth in spades. After a summer romance, Danny and Sandy end up at the same high school unbeknownst to each other. When mutual friends re-unite them at the school's first pep rally, Danny is ecstatic to see Sandy. But his friends give him funny looks when his excitement spills over. So he changes his demeanor to aloof and unfriendly.

The wrong friends can influence us on much deeper levels than merely how we act so we have social status or acceptability.

That night I made a choice not to be influenced by friends' choices anymore. They were co-workers that I saw every day, so pulling back was not a comfortable scenario. Thankfully, they knew me well enough not to take offense when I declined to go clubbing with them anymore. I changed jobs not long after. Every now and then, I wonder how their lives turned out. All I knew at the time was that I needed to execute an about-face.

Have you ever made such a determination? It's difficult, to say the least. It takes strength to stand up to friends that we like to be around, but change is necessary when harmful situations keep arising.

Later in my discipleship walk, I was surprised to discover that Jesus went to parties. I had operated under the assumption that hanging out with Christians meant that the party was over.

Forever.

The Backdrop of Abundance and Plenty

Most people don't expect to find Jesus at parties.

In John 7:37–38, we find Him at the Feast of the Booths in Judea. Still celebrated today, this feast is also referred to as the Fes-tival of Sukkot (Leviticus 23:34). Sukkot (pronounced sue-COAT) begins the fifth day after Yom Kippur (Leviticus 16:29–30). It's a drastic transition from one of the most solemn holidays in the

Jewish year to one of the most joyous. Sukkot is so unreservedly joyful that it's commonly referred to in Jewish prayer and literature as the Season of Rejoicing. Just imagine that party in Jesus' day; there were no legal or safety regulations in place like we have at national parties celebrated today.

Sukkot is the last of the three pilgrimage festivals. Like Passover and Shavu'ot (Leviticus 23:15–16), Sukkot has a dual significance: Historically, this particular opulent celebration commemorates the forty-year period during which the Israelites wandered in the desert, living in temporary shelters. Agriculturally, Sukkot is a harvest festival, sometimes referred to as the Festival of Ingathering.

It's significant to note that Jesus, the wellspring of life, attended a festival commemorating harvest time. Without water, there wouldn't be a harvest. Jesus strategically drew on that connection.

The word *sukkot* means "booths," and refers to the temporary dwellings that Jews were commanded to live in during this holiday in memory of the forty years of wandering. The name of the holiday is frequently translated "Feast of Tabernacles," which is misleading because the biblical word *tabernacle* was the word for God's dwelling place on earth. Sukkot lasts for seven days. No work is permitted on the first and second days of the festival, but it is permitted on the remaining days. It's important to put into perspective the historical significance of this greatly celebrated holiday because Jesus was about to reveal an even bigger reason to celebrate.

To reach the most people in one place at one time, Jesus situated Himself in the middle of this huge celebration.

Party Overload

Jesus arrived in Judea after the party was under way, but He didn't go straight to the celebration. He went to the temple and taught first. When He did head to the party, the celebration was on its last day.

Think about that for a moment.

65

After seven straight days of unreserved rejoicing, can you imagine the state of some partygoers? The people were living in temporary booths where, perhaps, the rules of home were relaxed. Maybe moral standards had been relaxed as well. Scripture calls this last celebration day "the great day," which indicates the party's climax.

Just imagine that scene. Today, it would be like attending the Mardi Gras celebrations in New Orleans. There were probably overindulgences of every kind, raucous behavior, excessive drinking, and more.

It's at that particular point, at the end of this grand party, that Jesus chooses to speak up:

> On the last day of the feast, the great day,
> Jesus stood up and cried out, "If anyone thirsts,
> let him come to Me and drink." John 7:37

He waited until the people had been partying for seven straight days before speaking. Jesus knew that despite their excesses, the people weren't filled. They were still thirsty. Not for regular water or wine, but for something they could not pinpoint. Some of the religious people may have recognized Jesus' reference to the promise given by God through Isaiah:

> And the LORD will guide you continually and
> satisfy your desire in scorched places and
> make your bones strong; and you shall be
> like a watered garden, like a spring of water,
> whose waters do not fail. Isaiah 58:11

The Lord promises to satisfy our desires in scorched places. In the original Hebrew, the phrase "in scorched places" means "in drought." It represents those dehydrated areas of our life where we build mental, emotional, and spiritual dams to shut out God's hydration. The reference fits perfectly for the party Jesus attended that day.

After indulging in a six-month season of partying, I understand precisely the soul thirst that Jesus referenced. I struggled to find my identity and looked to something other than Him. Simply put, I had chosen the wrong well to draw from. Looking for love in all the wrong places. (Great, that song won't leave my head now.)

At that point in my life, I didn't believe in Jesus or what He did on the cross. I thought His was a feel-good story made up by fanatics who believed in something so culturally irrelevant that it was laughable. I had decided that God was not who I needed. How could I when I couldn't even see Him?

Thanks, but no thanks.

I sought God only when I ran out of all other options. I used Him like a lucky rabbit's foot that I usually stuffed away in my pocket. Trouble? Take it out, give it a prayer rub, and keep making boneheaded decisions, expecting Him to bail me out.

Prayer occurred to me only when trouble came a-knocking. Talk about messed up.

Yet for some strange reason, I believed it was acceptable to utter those rabbit's foot prayers to God whenever I sat in the middle of a self-created mess. If He actually existed, I wanted Him to spare me the pain and reality of turning around and facing the wagonload of sin I kept dragging behind me.

When the Cultural Party Ends

Eventually, when our partying ends, we still have to face the accumulated baggage in our lives and the pain it generates.

Pain serves as one of the ways that God gets our attention. When we suffer enough, we begin looking for relief outside of the norm since the old remedies no longer work.

Naturally, that begs the question: Why would a loving God allow hurt, pain, and disappointment in our lives?

> My son, do not despise the LORD's discipline or
> be weary of His reproof, for the LORD reproves

him whom He loves, as a father the son in
whom he delights. Proverbs 3:11–12

Because God loves us. Simple as that.

My six-month clubbing stint provides vivid insights. I had repeatedly gotten myself into situations that could have easily harmed me on several levels; then God stepped in. I wasn't being a good steward of the gifts, talents, and abilities He had given me. I needed to learn.

And thanks to my hard head, I had to learn the hard way.

Not long into my new discipleship journey, I learned that God does not *cause* our suffering. He *allows* it.

He allows you and me to suffer the consequences of our own actions. Much like parents sometimes allow their children to deal with the ramifications of their choices in order to teach them. Those teachable moments promote maturity.

By God's grace, He doesn't abandon us to the messes we create.

You and I, by nature, drink from the wells that keep us dehydrated; we always will.

Apart from God's love and grace, revealed in Jesus, given to us by His Spirit, we would have nothing else to drink from.

Oasis or Desert?

In Israel, the Dead Sea is, well, dead. Since the saline content is extremely high, it contains no living organisms. It also stinks due to the decay and mineral content.

When I visited Israel a few years ago, our group's bus drove along the road that runs along the Dead Sea. Surrounded by desert as far as the eye can see, we could smell the putrid Dead Sea long before it ever came into view. Talk about double dehydration!

When our bus turned into Jericho, it was a feast for the eyes *and* nose. Jericho is an oasis. Literally. Springs hydrate Jericho from deep underground. Green trees, grass, and flowers delighted our parched senses.

Doesn't that paint an interesting picture of our spiritual life?

Jericho was the place of choice for travelers making their way to Jerusalem. Jesus and His disciples passed through there on several occasions (Matthew 20:29; Luke 18:35; Mark 10:46).

People are drawn to life-giving, hydrating places. Not many people intentionally visit a desert to unwind and relax.

Interestingly, though, an oasis appears only in a desert; one does not exist without the other. We find that same truth in light and dark. In lives surrendered to Christ and those that are not.

God's wellspring of life serves as the Christian's oasis in the desert of the world. In our journey through life, we are always traveling toward one or the other.

While passing through Jericho, Jesus met a tax collector named Zacchaeus. Zacchaeus was living high on the hog by milking the people through exorbitant taxes. He thought he had it all. Looked like he did too. Yet when Jesus appears on the scene, Zacchaeus's dehydration becomes very evident. He's so desperate to get a glimpse of Jesus that he climbs a tree—a very undignified act for a dignified rich man.

> He entered Jericho and was passing through. And behold, there was a man named Zacchaeus. He was a chief tax collector and was rich. And he was seeking to see who Jesus was, but on account of the crowd he could not, because he was small in stature. So he ran on ahead and climbed up into a sycamore tree to see Him, for He was about to pass that way. And when Jesus came to the place, He looked up and said to him, "Zacchaeus, hurry and come

down, for I must stay at your house today."
Luke 19:1–5

Zacchaeus was thirsty. Dehydrated. Empty. Although earthly things of comfort surrounded him, he abandoned them in favor of getting closer to the Wellspring of Life to ease the pain of his soul's dehydration.

We use possessions and addictions in vain to fill us when life feels empty. These things deceive us with a false promise of being enough. They can sure help you throw a great party. But that kind of party life leads us to the desert of dehydration.

Zacchaeus was running on the emptiness of worldly possessions. Jesus warns us against such pursuits: "one's life does not consist in the abundance of his possessions" (Luke 12:15).

If we're not careful, possessions or position replace relationships. You and I can love things, but things cannot love us back. Things are a great supplement to a full life, but a weak substitute for the right things in life. We find true contentment in Christ alone:

Not that I am speaking of being in need, for
I have learned in whatever situation I am to
be content. I know how to be brought low,
and I know how to abound. In any and every
circumstance, I have learned the secret of facing plenty and hunger, abundance and need.
Philippians 4:11–12

Before meeting Jesus, all Zacchaeus had were things. But encountering Jesus changed everything. He no longer cared how others perceived him. He needed a life change ASAP.

And thanks to God's grace, a better alternative had been revealed.

A Mirage or Reality?

As a new disciple, I'll bet you recognize the feeling. Zacchaeus lived in an oasis, but his worldly source of hydration was a mirage. During tough seasons of life, we may think that Jesus is a mirage. A hope that never materializes.

The desert sand of adversity or hurt swirls fast and blinds us for a time. But Jesus serves as our spiritual oasis. He remains ever present with us in our desert times to hydrate us despite the desert circumstances we are in. As His children, we are never without His hydration. His wellspring of life is unaffected by time and season. His life-giving promises are ever flowing and always present to satisfy every thirst. The good news is that no matter which river we jump into, God is ready to give us His river of living water. From Genesis to Revelation, we see Him faithfully redeem one sinner after another.

If we believe that Jesus died, was buried, and rose victorious from the grave to redeem us from our sins, then the Holy Spirit, that fountain of eternal life, dwells in us (John 4:10, 13–14).

Billy Graham put it this way:

> The Bible teaches that Satan is the author of sin. Sin is the reason that we have afflictions, including death. All of our problems and our suffering, including death itself, are a result of man's rebellion against God. But God has provided a rescue in the Person of His Son, Jesus Christ. That's why Christ died on the cross. That's why He rose from the dead.[2]

At the time that Jesus extended the invitation at Sukkot, believers had to wait to receive that full outpouring of the Holy Spirit until after His death (Romans 8:9). But since Jesus died more than two thousand years ago, you and I receive that full outpouring the moment we believe. Christ's death and resurrection proclaimed in the Gospel brings life to all who thirst for Him and His blessings.

Jesus did not attend that great party to party greatly. He went to make Himself available. He did not barge into the great party criticizing or alienating. He entered into the culture, observed, and then spoke. He excelled at reaching out to people in their own environment, where their guard was down.

We see that truth as Jesus met the Samaritan woman, when He met the invalid, when He welcomed Zacchaeus, and when He spoke to many others. Jesus mingled among the people. He wasn't waiting in a safe bubble, surrounded by like-minded people. He didn't wait for those people to get themselves into church before reaching out to them.

Jesus invited everyone—regardless of lifestyle, gender, or race—to drink from His living water. He didn't form exclusive cliques to minister only to His favorites.

He said, *"Whoever* believes in me" (John 7:38, emphasis added). That phrase conveys the measure of God's vast love for us. He desires that all of us spend eternity with Him in the mansions that Jesus prepared for us.

John Newton, who wrote the hymn "Amazing Grace," put it like this:

> When I was young, I was sure of many things; now there are only two things of which I am sure: one is, that I am a miserable sinner; and the other, that Christ is an all-sufficient Saviour.[3]

It took a significant amount of pain and heartache before I actually heard Jesus' invitation to partake of His living water. Perhaps you stand at the same crossroads now. Whether you are blind, lame, or paralyzed, He extends that same invitation to you.

It's the same one He extended to those Sukkot partygoers:

"If anyone thirsts, let him come to Me and drink." John 7:37

"Amazing grace ⁓ how sweet the sound."

A PAUSE AT THE WELL

Let's take a moment to pause for some practical application. Reflect on the life you led both before and after becoming a Christian and then answer these questions:

1. Have you ever led a party lifestyle? If so, what were the ups and downs of that lifestyle?

2. If you no longer party until you drop, why not?

3. How do you feel about the fact that Jesus attended parties?

4. Have you ever relied on possessions or pastimes to fill an inner emptiness? If so, what was the result?

5. Did you, like me, ever use God as a lucky rabbit's foot when bad choices landed you in difficulties? What happened?

None of us enjoys emotional, mental, or spiritual pain. However, it gets our attention to allow for spiritual growth and the maturing of our faith.

6. How has God used pain to alter the course of your life?

7. Have you shared with others the wisdom you gained from the experience?

Human nature is the author of sin, but God is the Author of life. And when it's all said and done, God wins. One day, all those who believe in what Jesus accomplished for mankind on the cross will spend eternity in God's glorious presence.

That truth lends perspective to how we spend our time on earth; are we dehydrated by worldly pursuits, or hydrated by the Wellspring of Life?

Are we living in an oasis or mirage?

. . . .

PRAYER STARTER

Take some time to ask God to identify friends in your life who may be leading you in directions away from Him. One by one, pray for each of them, and seek God's guidance about the future of those friendships.

. . . .

CHAPTER 4

GOD, I CAN SQUEEZE YOU IN THURSDAY AT EIGHT

As a deer pants for flowing streams, so pants my soul for You, O God. My soul thirsts for God, for the living God. ∼ Psalm 42:1–2

At eighty-five years old, Max Glauben's wrinkled arm still bears marks as a reminder of the nightmare he survived in his youth. He vividly remembers the terrible day that he, his family, and other Jews were rounded up and herded like cattle into a boxcar. The five-day train ride took them to Majdanek, a German concentration camp in Poland.

During those five hellish days, they were never let out of the boxcar and didn't receive food or water.

He remembers the boxcar's ceiling dripping from the collective humidity of their breath. He recalls, "You were hoping for a drop to fall on your lips so you can wet them, because it's much harder to die of dehydration than it is from starvation."

Max was the only one from his family who survived to tell the story.

In our comfortable, twenty-first-century lives, we can hardly imagine such an experience. We may hear about atrocities on the evening news, but those things occur in developing countries halfway around the globe. Those events don't noticeably affect our daily lives.

However, we certainly understand thirst. Without physical hydration, we know we will die.

But what about hydration for our soul?

As a young adult, I didn't understand such a concept. I operated under the assumption that if I had everything I desired externally, then all would be well internally.

When I turned twenty, I moved into my own apartment and went after everything the world had to offer. Although we were not poor growing up, we did not have many extras. So I set my sights on grabbing all of the things I believed the world owed to me.

Since I was overly concerned about how others perceived me, I wanted to appear as a successful, well-rounded modern-day woman. My entry-level job couldn't support such a lifestyle, but I didn't let such a trifle slow me down.

Using my credit cards and checkbook as if I had thousands of dollars in the bank, I soon ran into serious trouble. I maxed out my credit cards, ran out of money, and could not pay the rent. I began writing bad checks to cover my horrible spending habits. I regularly missed car payments, believing that the car loan company would somehow be lenient and put up with my lame excuses. I floated bad checks for groceries since I'd spent all my money on material possessions that I thought I needed.

Of course that lifestyle didn't last long. The finance company repossessed my car, and the grocery store, where I floated the bad checks, sent the county sheriff after me to collect the debts.

And for what?

To live a life I couldn't afford that would ensure that everyone thought I was better off than I was? Better than them? It fed my ego to hear friends say that they wished they could live the life I was living. Well, I learned the hard way that gloating is a lot like bloating: you fill up on yourself and it makes you nauseous.

Jesus wove a similar story in Scripture featuring a man and his two sons. The prodigal son was tired of rural life and wanted a taste of the big wide world, on his own terms:

> There was a man who had two sons. And the younger of them said to his father, "Father, give me the share of property that is coming to me." And he divided his property between them. Not many days later, the younger son gathered all he had and took a journey into a far country, and there he squandered his property in reckless living. And when he had spent everything, a severe famine arose in that country, and he began to be in need. So he went and hired himself out to one of the citizens of that country, who sent him into his

fields to feed pigs. And he was longing to be
fed with the pods that the pigs ate, and no one
gave him anything. Luke 15:11–16

This story had a powerful impact on me when I became a Christian because it was *my* journey. Well, all except the part about starting with an inheritance. Mine started with arrogance and ignorance and spiraled down from there.

The word *prodigal* means "wasteful." Was there a time in your life when, like me, you were careless? If your answer is yes, then I want you to know that there's hope.

Just to let you know, the word *prodigal* also means "recklessly extravagant." Before you think all is lost, there is no part of our life that God cannot redeem. His love is recklessly extravagant toward His children. Although we mess up, there is nothing we confess that makes Jesus love us any less.

Living the grand life may have been fun to brag about, but looking back, I realize that my friends were smarter. They weren't wasteful or reckless. They lived within their means, took care of their bills, and put money into savings.

Like the prodigal son, I longed after something far greater than pods or husks could satisfy; it was a thirst that no earthly fountain could slake. But I had chosen the wrong well from which to drink.

I grew up in a loving family with parents who cherished my sisters and me. I was never mistreated, and I never went without a basic need being met. I was just an entitled, self-indulgent knucklehead.

Eventually I swallowed my pride and asked my parents if I could come home. I gave up the lease on my apartment and moved back in with them. And I slowly began digging my way out of debt.

Although my parents lovingly welcomed me back home with open arms, I'll never forget the look of pain in their eyes. They wanted to spare me the heartache from the mess I'd created, but they knew it was a lesson that I needed to learn through experience.

Perhaps that's why the prodigal son's father gave him his inheritance early.

Sometimes, hardheaded fools just have to learn the hard way.

My behavior was similar to my asking God for a motorcycle at three years old. God knew I wasn't ready, emotionally or spiritually, to handle the world's disarray on my own without creating chaos. Yet, because He loved me, God allowed that painful time in my life to teach me lessons that I've never forgotten.

When the prodigal son came to his senses in that pig field, he swallowed his pride and came up with a plan to return home and work for his father like a hired servant:

> When he came to himself, he said, "How many of my father's hired servants have more than enough bread, but I perish here with hunger! I will arise and go to my father, and I will say to him, 'Father, I have sinned against heaven and before you. I am no longer worthy to be called your son. Treat me as one of your hired servants.'" And he arose and came to his father. Luke 15:17–20

The prodigal son is thirsty for reconciliation. We realize just how soul-thirsty he is when we understand three important points in these verses:

- He realized that, above all, he had sinned against heaven. Against God. His heavenly Father had provided the prodigal son with many blessings, including an earthly father who knew how to manage his livelihood. In all likelihood, the son would not have asked his father for his inheritance in the first place if the resources hadn't been available.

- He realized that his dehydrated, worldly desires not only affected his earthly father, but his brother as well.

- He set his mind on asking his father if he could return as a hired servant, not as a son. Not even as a house servant, but as a hired servant. Hired servants had to make their own way to survive. House servants lived under the master's roof and were provided with food and a place to sleep. But the son didn't ask his father for the slightest courtesy that might cost his father any money. He would be content as a hired servant if his father would take him back. His soul thirsted for a restored relationship with his father and he was willing to work for it.

The prodigal son understands that he is no longer worthy to be called a son. Sonship isn't based on worth; it's based on birth. When you and I are born into the kingdom of God, we have been birthed as God's sons and daughters. God has prepared for us a heavenly inheritance because of that birth, not because of our worth. We will never be worthy, but Christ's sacrifice on the cross paid our sin debt. His extravagant love for us paved the way for us to be birthed into an eternal kingdom.

It's about birth, not worth.

In this parable, Jesus paints a portrait of a loving father who forgives his child's sin to welcome him home. When you and I mess up, when our worldly thirst leads us to wells that shrivel and dehydrate us, God still welcomes us back with open arms. We see that parallel in the prodigal son's return:

> But while he was still a long way off, his father saw him and felt compassion, and ran and embraced him and kissed him. . . . "Bring quickly the best robe, and put it on him, and put a ring on his hand, and shoes on his feet. And bring the fattened calf and kill it, and let us eat and celebrate. For this my son was dead, and is alive again; he was lost, and is found." And they began to celebrate. Luke 15:20, 22–24

The father relentlessly scanned the horizon, looking for his lost son. He desired to repair and embrace that broken relationship with his son. He never gave up hoping.

And God never gives up on us. Although we may run away from His wellspring, believing we know what's best, He still longs to give us a drink from His river of life-giving water. When our spiritual well is dry, leaving us panting from thirst, no water but God's wellspring of life satisfies.

It's that same panting that King David references in Psalm 42:

> As a deer pants for flowing streams, so pants my soul for You, O God. Psalm 42:1

The word picture David paints is one of running a race with everything we've got. Full out, nothing held back. He compares the deer's yearning for water to sustain physical life to his soul's need for the living God, the source of spiritual life.

Panting refers to desiring in a state of exhaustion. If we have reached a state of panting, we can conclude that we've already been exerting ourselves.

But to what end?

More often than I care to admit, I choose exerting my time and energy toward circumstantial comfort or happiness.

Thankfully, God calls us into bigger stories than the ones we write for ourselves. Scripture tells us specifically what we are to long for as His children:

> Yes, LORD, walking in the way of Your laws, we
> wait for You; Your name and renown are the
> desire of our hearts. My soul yearns for You
> in the night; in the morning my spirit longs for
> You. Isaiah 26:8–9 (NIV)

Can you honestly say that God is the ultimate desire of your heart today? your soul's most desperate need?

Far too often, I fall far short of the mark, exhausting myself with the things of the world. Suffocating schedules seem to rule the day.

But toward what goal?

When you view your schedule, what comprises the lion's share of your time? Those who work in the corporate world spend most of their waking hours at work. But what about when the workday is over? Today's technologically advanced world offers us the opportunity to stay connected with work 24/7.

How often do you see parents checking e-mail at their child's sports game?

We have the choice between allowing ourselves to maintain that frantic pace or letting the technology rest so we can connect with family and friends in real time. But often our addiction to busyness dehydrates us from the soul out.

Another noteworthy point in Psalm 42:1 is the fact that our *soul* pants for God. Not our heart or mind, but our soul.

The Hebrew word for "soul" used here is *nephesh*, which refers to our whole self, our whole being, every physical and spiritual aspect of our lives. Our soul is the seat of our passions, emotions, appetites, and desires. It is through our soul that God draws us toward Him in relationship.

With those volatile senses residing in our soul, it's crucial that God alone meets and sanctifies our needs and longings. When we look to other sources or people to fill them, we end up in a world of trouble.

When I went through my turbulent early years, those misplaced longings translated into looking for love in clubs. Looking for acceptance through buying people's attention and affections. Both paths led to dehydrated living.

I learned the hard way that bending my knees in surrender to God proves difficult as long as I stubbornly remained standing in endless battles for significance. Pride and many other attitudes hinder that simple surrender. Sometimes we try something else, anything else. I certainly did. Eventually, through a significant amount of pain resulting from bad decisions, I realized that self-hydration never works.

When I turn back toward God, I find Him still giving me a drink from His wellspring.

He's inviting you too!

The Living God

Psalm 42:2 states, "My soul thirsts for God, for the living God." Only God can satisfy our soul thirst. Not just any god, the *living* God. The psalmist emphasizes that truth because in biblical times, many worshiped idols and false gods.

Not much has changed over the centuries.

The Hebrew word used to reference God here is *Elohim*, which refers to the one true, eternal, self-sustained Existence—the monotheistic God of Israel. He is the one true God. Always available. Never changing:

I the Lord do not change. Malachi 3:6

Every good and perfect gift is from above,
coming down from the Father of the heavenly

> lights, who does not change like shifting shad-
> ows. James 1:17 (NIV)

He is the one who created all and sustains all. And He created us to be in relationship with Him. We serve a living, loving God whom our soul thirsts after.

Thirst is one of the most powerful spiritual symbols in Scripture. As dehydration draws the whole of our physical being to long for water, so God draws our soul to long for deeper meaning to life.

How does our soul thirst? What does that even look like?

Our soul bears the burdens of life's trials. At times, don't you feel battered from the inside out? Oftentimes, especially in times of grief, our soul thirsts after God's comfort. We do not thirst after a well that dries up! He is fully present in every generation—from the beginning to the end of time. When we thirst after God, we find our living God and Soul Quencher seated firmly on His throne, ready to pour out His refreshment into dry, parched souls.

Banishing the Myth

When we struggle with parched areas of our life, some people like to spout one particular pet, Christian-ese phrase: "God will never give you more than you can handle."

Many Christians hold to this as absolute truth. Actually, it's an absolute myth. It's a dehydrating lie meant to make us feel better when the going gets tough.

If God will never give us more than we can handle, then what do we need Him for? We probably hear that pet phrase most often when someone we know is living in a rough season in life. Has someone ever said it to you? How did you receive it?

When I was going through my divorce, I heard that phrase often. Honestly, it made me want to kick the person who said it. Hard.

All of us face times in our lives when we have been overwhelmed. Sometimes it's our own doing. Sometimes it isn't. But

ALL the time, feeling overwhelmed feels like spinning out of control. Like you've lost the grip on keeping the pieces of your life from being sucked away in an F5 tornado. Then some well-meaning person comes along, with sincerity in her eyes, grabs your arm to ensure she's got your full attention, and then lays that line on you.

Sheesh.

Talk about a dehydrating phrase that does nothing to sooth our hurting soul. Those words are not welcoming or comforting. In fact, they often serve to create discouragement that the hurting person can't seem to control his or her life.

But most of all, that phrase isn't true. God never said it. Jesus never taught it.

So where did it come from? The apostle Paul's First Letter to the Church in Corinth reminded the people that everyone is tempted, yet often chooses to do the wrong thing. Paul's warning addresses the reality of temptation and sin that confronts us every day. But his warning came with a promise:

> No temptation has overtaken you except what
> is common to mankind. And God is faithful; He
> will not let you be tempted beyond what you
> can bear. But when you are tempted, He will
> also provide a way out so that you can endure
> it. 1 Corinthians 10:13 (NIV)

This verse, often misquoted, is where that phrase originated. Paul states that we'll never be tempted beyond what we can bear. But he doesn't suggest that WE have the strength to overcome all temptations in our own strength. Paul states that GOD faithfully provides us the strength needed to resist and be victorious.

Paul specifically addressed temptation—not suffering, illness, pain, or affliction. With temptation, you can choose to give in to it or rely on God's strength to resist it. But with suffering and other hardships, you often don't have a choice. They come into your life without notice or warning.

But that's only part of the problem. The misquote implies that WE can handle the situation on our own. That's just not true. When we feel overwhelmed, we need to know that Jesus knows exactly how we feel.

In the Garden of Gethsemane, the night before Jesus was crucified, He cried out:

> My soul is overwhelmed with sorrow to the point of death. Matthew 26:38 (NIV)

Jesus was admitting to His Father that in His mortal, humble state, He could not bear such a great burden.

Even Jesus knows what overwhelmed feels like. That uniquely qualifies Him as our ultimate comforter. It's okay to feel as if we can't handle our situation. We cry out to God, remembering that His promises extend to us through the person of Jesus: "I am with you always" (Matthew 28:20); "I will never leave you nor forsake you" (Hebrews 13:5).

When we pant after God's living water of comfort, when we are suffering and remember His promises, we will find Jesus right there in our time of need. He's there with us in the hospital room. In divorce court. At the cemetery. In the unemployment office. In the prison cell of addiction.

Right there with us at all times.

We Can't Handle It, But God Can

When life gives us more than we can handle, I suggest using this new phrase: *"God will never give us more than HE can handle!"*

When our soul thirsts and pants after Him, He doesn't head in the other direction. He is right there with us. He meets us in our mess, pain, hardship, and suffering. And when He does, we learn to recognize our constant need to depend on Him and partake of His living water.

Making room for God in our pre-existing, personal-comfort-zone-designed box promotes the myth that God will not give us anything more than we can handle.

God didn't come to reside in our box.

He came to offer us a heavenly mansion.

God has demonstrated in no uncertain terms His willingness to be a part of our mess, to be with us, and to provide the help that we need. He did all that by coming down to earth in the person of Jesus Christ. He knew that our sin was something that we couldn't handle—even on our best days. Even when we're playing our A-game.

He knows that we have no way to get ourselves out of our sin situation.

We cannot handle it, but He can.

And He did.

Jesus' sacrifice provided God's checkmate to sin.

Jesus took our place by obeying the Law to the letter. He took our place in punishment for sin. He took our place on that cross. And He conquered death so that we could live forever with Him.

All we have to do is repent and believe God's faithful promises.

And as He does when He quenches our thirsty souls, God has many ways to offer refreshment. When we struggle, God may handle it by sending to us someone who will walk through it beside us. Being receptive to those helpers whom God sends into our life is essential, whether they are pastors, counselors, friends, or family.

Sometimes you are the person God sends to walk with someone while they are struggling, suffering, hurting, and feeling overwhelmed. That is your chance to show Jesus' love and compassion. To be with them in the midst of suffering. To help another carry the weight, burden, and load:

> Carry each other's burdens, and in this way
> you will fulfill the law of Christ. Galatians 6:2
> (NIV)

All it takes is for us, as followers of Jesus, to demonstrate the love and care of Christ to another individual.

Changing the world isn't accomplished all at once in grand gestures. It happens one life at a time. One divine appointment at a time. It happens when we show God's care to our neighbor:

> Let each of you look not only to his own
> interests, but also to the interests of others.
> Philippians 2:4

> Truly, I say to you, as you did it to one of the
> least of these my brothers, you did it to me.
> Matthew 25:40

Talk about soul hydration!

Go Ahead and Celebrate

Like the prodigal son, we have messed up in life.

When his senses returned to him, he approached his father with a step-by-step plan to restore their relationship, based on worth instead of birth. But the prodigal son's father, mirroring our heavenly Father, absorbed the son's full debt and extended grace and forgiveness. To the son's surprise, the father ordered his son to be cleaned up, given new clothes, and special jewelry. He ordered the servants to kill the fattened calf for a feast that would celebrate his child's return.

Did you ever stop to wonder how the son felt at that moment? What did the son have to celebrate about?

His behavior? Nothing to celebrate about.

His wise financial investments? Again, nothing to celebrate about.

There's only one reason that kid could celebrate: *because his dad still loved him.*

Sometimes we thirst after the wrong well and our lives end up in one big mess. But our heavenly Father scans the horizon, waiting for us to return. He's eager to celebrate our homecoming with a party in our honor. To restore our relationship with Him. To drink from His soul-hydrating wellspring of life.

How do we know we'll be able to enjoy that celebration?

Because our heavenly Father still loves us.

Despite what we've done.

A PAUSE AT THE WELL

Let's take a moment to pause for some practical application.

God longs to quench our thirst in every area of our lives. But surrendering and repenting comes first. Believing that God only moves into the part in our lives where we choose to make room for Him shouts absurdity. God didn't send Jesus to fit in. He sent Jesus to sacrifice His all to the will of the Father.

1. If God asks that of His Son, would He ask anything less of us?

But you and I both know that repentance and surrender can be uncomfortable. *Very uncomfortable.* It means handing over the controls of your life, lock, stock, and barrel (to use a down-home, Texas phrase). That means that we will face brokenness (mostly our pride and self-adoration) and encounter situations way beyond our capabilities.

But surrender is absolutely necessary.

2. What are some circumstances in your life right now—personal, work related, ministry related, relational, and so forth—where you long for God's wellspring of joy and abundance?

. . . .

PRAYER STARTER

*Take some time to thank God for gifting us with His
joy. Then, for those areas in your life you identified above,
ask God to identify the roadblocks that have been erected
that are robbing you of living in His joy. One by one,
pray that God remove each of them and lead you back
to His joyful wellspring.*

. . . .

CHAPTER 5

WATER CONNECTIONS

What shall we say then? Are we to continue in sin that grace may abound? By no means! How can we who died to sin still live in it? Do you not know that all of us who have been baptized into Christ Jesus were baptized into His death? We were buried therefore with Him by baptism into death, in order that, just as Christ was raised from the dead by the glory of the Father, we too might walk in newness of life. ∼ Romans 6:1–4

It was Palm Sunday of 1991.

My hands trembled as they gripped the steering wheel. The countryside blurred outside the car windows as I sped to church. I was running late. Again.

Anxiety pounded hard in my chest. Not because I was running behind schedule, but because today was about taking a leap of faith into the waters of Baptism.

Six months before, I had willingly walked into a church for Sunday morning service at the invitation of a new friend. My freak-o-meter was off the charts. I didn't know the people, routine, or what was expected of me.

I sat rigid during the whole service, waiting for the Church People to pounce on me. To judge me. To tell me I wasn't good enough to be in the Christian club. I held my bulletin like a shield in front of me to ward off attacks.

I realize that's not fair, kind, or flattering, but that was my reality. My level of fear was pegging off the charts, but I couldn't figure out why. I didn't like fear. It felt like wearing a heavy winter coat in the desert.

Then, over the six months that followed my initial church visit, I noticed subtle changes. My freak-o-meter no longer topped the charts every time I approached the church's front doors. The Church People were so kind and loving that I began to look forward to Sunday mornings.

When my friend asked if I had been baptized, I confessed that I hadn't. After explaining what that meant and confirming my willingness to be baptized, he made the appropriate arrangements with the pastors.

I attended a twelve-week adult confirmation class to learn more about God, the Church, and the faith to which He had called me.

Then the big day arrived.

Since my Baptism would take place in front of the congregation, I was much more concerned about what I would wear and how I looked than the supernatural exchange that would take place. (I'm so thankful that God calls us out of our shallowness into the deep waters of His love.)

On that beautiful Palm Sunday, my Baptism day, I remember the senior pastor reciting this verse:

> We were therefore buried with Him through baptism into death in order that, just as Christ was raised from the dead through the glory of the Father, we too may live a new life.
> Romans 6:4 (NIV)

That day, my old self (the old Adam) was drowned in Baptism—buried with Christ—and my new self emerged with Christ. I didn't fully understand the significance of that day or event then. But God provided the faith for me to believe that just as Jesus was raised from the dead and now lives exalted in the fullness of His divine nature, I, too, live a new life.

What's the Big Deal About Baptism?

Baptism doesn't make us physically appear any different. We gain something far greater than outward change, more powerful and infinitely incomprehensible—the gift of the Holy Spirit living inside of us for all eternity:

> And Peter said to them, "Repent and be baptized every one of you in the name of Jesus Christ for the forgiveness of your sins, and you will receive the gift of the Holy Spirit. For the promise is for you and for your children and for all who are far off, everyone whom the Lord our God calls to Himself." Acts 2:38–39

Living a new life in Christ means we no longer have to live for ourselves. We no longer have to live according to our past. We live according to God's promises in the present and with certain hope for the future. Our old self must be buried with Christ in

His death in order that we might be raised with Him in His resurrection and live as Christ lives: for God and not for ourselves (see Romans 6:10).

Baptism isn't simply a ceremony we perform. God is the one who works and acts in Baptism. Through His actions, we receive His grace and His good gifts. This is the promise and starting point from which God leads us on our spiritual journey.

If you were baptized as an infant, your parents followed God's mandate as your spiritual guardians to have you baptized. If you were baptized as an adult, like me, God drew you to Himself.

Some may believe that it takes months of weighing the pros and cons before getting baptized. But we're not deciding if we're going to move to Tibet and take a lifelong vow of silence. Baptism is a clear instruction from God by which He gives us His grace and forgiveness and that serves as a catalyst for a changed life in us. Changes that can make an eternal difference, not just for us, but for others.

Before we can be leaders of people, we have to be followers of Christ. And if we're going to follow, we need to heed His call, obey His instruction, and be raised to new life through the waters of Baptism.

More than that, we need what Baptism offers: forgiveness for when we don't obey and the blessings of the Holy Spirit so that we might follow in faith wherever our Savior leads.

Baptism: The Origin

Baptism as we know it first appeared in the first-century Church. It originates out of Jesus' teaching to the disciples:

> Go therefore and make disciples of all nations,
> baptizing them in the name of the Father and
> of the Son and of the Holy Spirit, teaching
> them to observe all that I have commanded
> you. And behold, I am with you always, to the
> end of the age. Matthew 28:19–20

Wherever churches are planted, wherever people embrace Jesus, there is Baptism. But the manner by which it gets carried out among the world's denominations varies greatly.

Some denominations believe it's better to immerse people in water; others believe it's better to sprinkle it on their forehead. Some believe Baptism is our decision once we have weighed all the facts; others believe it is something God does and therefore is appropriate and essential for infants.

But all Christians agree that if you follow Christ, you must be baptized.

Period.

As a new disciple, it's important to understand where Baptism originated. The Greek word used in Scripture for "baptize" is *baptizō* (pronounced bap-TEE-zo). When Greek scholars translated the Bible into English, they used a **one-for-one translation**. In others words, when they saw the word *theos*, they recorded the word "God." One whole word for another whole word.

But there were some cases when, out of a lack of clear understanding and an existing Greek word with similar meaning, Bible scholars used a letter-by-letter translation called **transliteration.** *Baptizō* was one of those transliterated words.

Baptizō was a very common word in Greek culture that didn't carry the religious connotations that the English language has attached to it. In Greek literature, *baptizō* meant "to wash, plunge, soak, or dip," and it was used to describe people who drowned, ships that sank, and sometimes just the processing of washing something.

Here's one of the most famous uses of the word *baptizō*:

> The clearest example that shows the meaning of *baptizo* is a text from the Greek poet and physician Nicander, who lived about 200 B.C. It is a recipe for making pickles and is helpful because it uses both words. Nicander says that

in order to make a pickle, the vegetable should first be "dipped" (baptô) into boiling water and then "baptised" (baptizô) in the vinegar solution. Both verbs concern the immersing of vegetables in a solution. But the first is temporary. The second, the act of baptising the vegetable, produces a permanent change.[4]

Obviously, when you and I are baptized today, we assign the ritual a much deeper meaning than making pickles.

But where it becomes confusing is when the Greek translators sometimes translate the word *baptizō* as "wash" while other times they transliterate it to "baptize." Just a few examples from Scripture where *baptizō* isn't transliterated into "baptize" occur include:

And when they come from the marketplace, they do not eat unless they **wash** [*baptizō*]. And there are many other traditions that they observe, such as the **washing** [*baptizō*] of cups and pots and copper vessels and dining couches. Mark 7:4 (emphasis added)

The Pharisee was astonished to see that He did not first **wash** [*baptizō*] before dinner. Luke 11:38 (emphasis added)

So *baptizō* was a very common word. Understanding that prompts us to ask, how in the world did a very common word take on such significant religious connotation and meaning? What happened?

I'm glad you asked!

In Old Testament times, several hundred years before Jesus was born, when Gentiles (that is, non-Jewish people) interacted with Jews, they noticed that the Jews worshiped only one God. Some Gentiles agreed with the Jewish point of view, so they would attend the Jewish temples and worship in the outer court and visit Jewish synagogues.

Eventually, some Gentiles asked if they could become Jewish so they could fully embrace and follow the teachings of Yahweh (God). So the Jews came up with a process for a non-Jewish person to become Jewish.

Although different cultures came up with different requirements over the course of time, five main components made up the basic list: circumcision, a covenant meal, acknowledgment of the Law (the Law of God as revealed to Moses), a sacrifice, and a ceremonial washing.

The ceremonial washing was something done alone, in private. No one washed you. This ceremony symbolically represented the Gentile washing away and cleansing himself of sin and the old ways of life so he could become new and embrace the teachings of Judaism and identify with the God of the Jews.

Guess what word the Greek cultures assigned to that cleansing process? You guessed it, *baptizō*. They differentiated the word from "washing" by inserting an article in front of it to denote a ceremonial process that had religious connotations. When people saw those words together, they automatically associated it with something greater than regular washing.

So how did Baptism become something mandated for all Christians?

Again, I'm glad you asked.

Enter Jesus.

Jesus Changed Everything

In AD 30, a strange man who wore odd clothes appeared on the scene by the Jordan River and began preaching about repentance.

John the Baptist taught his listeners that God was getting ready to do something extraordinary in their midst. Something that had never been done before. He warned them to stop sinning and confess their sins because if they weren't right with God, they would miss what God was about to unfold.

Then he waded into the Jordan River and told them:

> I baptize you with water for repentance, but He who is coming after me is mightier than I, whose sandals I am not worthy to carry. He will baptize you with the Holy Spirit and fire.
> Matthew 3:11

As John the Baptist preached, the Jews would line up to be baptized. Now, we don't have pictures that show us exactly how he baptized people. However, whatever he did conveyed to the people that what was taking place carried a much greater significance than merely washing to remove outer dirt. It appeared to the Jews as some sort of ceremonial washing, so when the scribes recorded what John the Baptist was doing, they used the word *baptizō* along with the required article to convey that meaning.

Consequently, based on their understanding of ceremonial washing, such as when a Gentile became a Jew, the Jews associated John's actions with his message—that somehow, through that ceremonial washing, they were becoming something different than they were before.

So the Jews named him "John the Baptist." But that word for "Baptist" in the Greek (*baptistēs*) appears only in Christian literature. It means that when people saw what John the Baptist was doing, they didn't have a word for it, so they came up with a new one. That tells us that the word originated from the ceremonial washing that John was performing. All fourteen times *baptistēs* appears in the New Testament, it singularly refers to one who administers the rite of Baptism.

When the people lined up to be baptized by John, they were making a public declaration that they agreed with what he was teaching. Being baptized was a response to the call to repent.

And then one day, the One whom John told them was coming actually showed up:

> The next day he saw Jesus coming toward him, and said, "Behold, the Lamb of God, who takes away the sin of the world!" John 1:29

Then Jesus shocked John the Baptist by asking to be baptized. John tried to argue, saying how he wasn't worthy to even tie Jesus' sandals, but Jesus insisted:

> John would have prevented Him, saying, "I need to be baptized by You, and do You come to me?" But Jesus answered him, "Let it be so now, for thus it is fitting for us to fulfill all righteousness." Then he consented. Matthew 3:14–15

By allowing John the Baptist to baptize Him, Jesus was affirming His connection to sinful man. As the Son of Man, in His Baptism, Jesus began His ministry by publicly showing Himself to be one of us. The culmination of His ministry took place on the cross, where He became one of us (though without sin) by taking on our sin and suffering in our place.

As Jesus and His disciples traveled over the next three years to spread the hope of the Gospel, Jesus instructed His followers to baptize people who professed faith in His teachings. By their Baptism, the people displayed a public confession as followers of Christ and, more important, received the blessings of forgiveness, life, and salvation won for them by Him.

Jesus made clear that Baptism is an essential part of making disciples. So how does that translate to the New Testament Church today?

I really love your questions!

Baptism and the Holy Spirit

The moment when Jesus stood up in the tomb on Easter morning, forever defeating death for every believer, proved to be the ultimate game changer. When He rose from the grave, you and I were provided with the hope of being raised to life with Him into eternity through the ministry of the Holy Spirit.

After His resurrection, Jesus appeared to the disciples to tell them that He would send the Holy Spirit on Pentecost so His presence would reside in every believer:

> When the day of Pentecost arrived, they were all together in one place. And suddenly there came from heaven a sound like a mighty rushing wind, and it filled the entire house where they were sitting. And divided tongues as of fire appeared to them and rested on each one of them. And they were all filled with the Holy Spirit and began to speak in other tongues as the Spirit gave them utterance. Acts 2:1–4

So Peter, the apostle to the Jews in the New Testament Church, addressed the religious crowds after this extraordinary event to explain what had happened:

> Peter, standing with the eleven, lifted up his voice and addressed them: "Men of Judea and all who dwell in Jerusalem, let this be known to you, and give ear to my words. For these people are not drunk, as you suppose, since it is only the third hour of the day. But this is what was uttered through the prophet Joel: 'And in the last days it shall be, God declares, that I will pour out My Spirit on all flesh.'"
> Acts 2:14–17

It was an assurance, not vague. It continues:

> Now when they heard this they were cut to
> the heart, and said to Peter and the rest of the
> apostles, "Brothers, what shall we do?" And
> Peter said to them, "Repent and be baptized
> every one of you in the name of Jesus Christ
> for the forgiveness of your sins, and you will re-
> ceive the gift of the Holy Spirit." Acts 2:37–38

As it did with the Early Church, the gift of the Holy Spirit empowers us and strengthens us to follow God regardless of our circumstances. When you and I operate in the assurance that the One
who lives inside of us triumphs and claims victory over any and
every sin and addiction in our lives, sin will never claim victory
over our life again.

Now *that's* living water!

God made that promise to everyone, not only to those who try
to get their act together before coming to Him.

Nothing empowers us to get our act together better than the
Holy Spirit inside us, doing the spiritual housecleaning. You and
I will never be good enough or worthy of the incredible gift that
God offers through Baptism. That's why He offers it to ALL at no
cost—no behavior layaway required to receive the gift of the Holy
Spirit:

> The promise is for you and for your children
> and for all who are far off, everyone whom the
> Lord our God calls to Himself. Acts 2:39

ALL.

As Peter pleaded with those gathered that day, I plead with
you today: if you've never been baptized, in faith, come to the life-
giving water of Baptism and receive all that God has promised.
This isn't pressuring; it's pleading. "Pressuring" means that some-

how your actions benefit me. I am pleading with you for YOUR sake, not mine.

Baptism establishes the relationship that will become our foundation. Part of that relationship comes in the form of our repentance, just like John the Baptist preached. God already knows our sin, but confession takes away pride and leads to vulnerability, which leads to intimacy with God. We learn to trust Him.

Our confession is for our benefit, not His.

Baptism establishes the relationship and brings the blessings of forgiveness that give us confidence to come vulnerably before the throne of God.

Think back to when you were a child and you did something really bad. If you thought your parents would disown you and kick you out, then you were less likely to confess wrongdoing. On the other hand, if you knew you were unconditionally loved and nothing could keep your parents from having you as their child, then you found it easier to confess.

The supernatural act of Baptism guarantees God's love for us (sealed by the Spirit) and leads to a life of confession and forgiveness that turns us away from a life of sin to a life with Jesus.

Being raised to new life through the waters of Baptism isn't about showing ourselves as perfect to a world we want to impress. It's about tapping into God's wellspring of life and telling a lost and hurting world about a perfect Savior who died to give us eternal life.

A PAUSE AT THE WELL

Let's take a moment to pause for some practical application.

First things first: if you and/or your family member(s) have not been baptized, begin making the necessary arrangements to do so as soon as possible. The methods by which various religions carry out the act of Baptism does not detract from the power of what God accomplishes in that supernatural transaction.

1. Through Baptism, we receive God's grace and His good gifts. Take a moment to write your definition of *grace*. Don't look it up, just state what you think it is.

2. Now look up the word *grace*. Did your answer differ? How?

3. Part of our relationship with God comes in the form of our repentance. What does that word mean to you? Is it a regular practice in your discipleship journey?

4. Confession leads to vulnerability, which leads to intimacy with God. When is the last time you spent time alone with God in confession? How did that time impact your relationship with God?

* * * * * * * * * * * * * * * * * * * *

PRAYER STARTER

Take some time to ask God to identify those patterns or behaviors in your life that you need to repent of. One by one, confess each one, and receive His forgiveness.

* * * * * * * * * * * * * * * * * * * *

CHAPTER 6

DUDE, YOU'RE GOING TO NEED A COMPASS

"Make yourself an ark of gopher wood.... For behold, I will bring a flood of waters upon the earth to destroy all flesh in which is the breath of life under heaven. Everything that is on the earth shall die. But I will establish My covenant with you, and you shall come into the ark, you, your sons, your wife, and your son's wives with you."... Noah did this; he did all that God commanded him.

~ Genesis 6:14, 17–18, 22

The first time someone gifted me with a Bible, I smiled politely and thanked him. On the inside, I thought, *Am I supposed to read that whole thing? Look how thick it is!*

When I wasn't carrying it to impress the Church People on Sundays, my new Bible sat strategically on my coffee table. Of course it was just for show, to prove to guests I was a Christian. I guess following that logic, displaying a quantum physics book would prove I was a scientist.

But I wasn't bothered by such simple logic.

As the weeks following my new church membership progressed, one question blared in my mind louder than all the rest: *So, I'm a Christian. Now what?*

I felt stupid asking such a question. And asking one of the Church People was not an option. I didn't want my ignorance confirmed.

What I needed was an instruction manual, compass, or something to provide direction for this Christian journey. I started combing bookstores to find the perfect Christian "how-to" book. One Sunday, after weeks of half-hearted searching, I finally got up the nerve to ask a new friend at church what book she would recommend.

She looked down at the Bible resting in my hands, smiled, and said, "You're holding it."

Great. I'm going to have to read this whole book after all.

When I arrived home, following lunch and my usual nap, I brewed a fresh pot of coffee, settled on the couch, and picked up my Bible.

Even though I experienced a flash of resignation, I couldn't suppress a growing sense of expectation.

That afternoon began an incredible journey I never anticipated.

At first, reading the Bible was intimidating. I didn't know the first thing about Scripture or where to start. I discovered there was an Old Testament and a New Testament. I tabbed the "Table of Contents" page and forged ahead.

The Bible seemed so confusing. The account of creation was riveting, but Leviticus slowed me down. Then the Book of Numbers brought my reading to a complete halt. Cultures described there were several thousand years old and seemed far removed from modern-day application. I kept thinking, *How is this relevant?*

My twentieth-century mind could not wrap around the Old Testament animal sacrifices. Or the Israelites following Moses around in the desert for forty years. *Seriously?* I kept thinking that someone else should have handled the navigation. But continuing to read showed me that God had a specific plan for why those things took place, so I kept plowing ahead.

Some days it sure felt like plowing.

Initially, studying the Bible proved confusing, even frustrating for me. If that describes you too, here's what you need to know: It's okay. That's perfectly normal. Keep seeking. Keep digging. God promises:

> You will seek Me and find Me, when you seek
> Me with all your heart. Jeremiah 29:13

Eventually, I reached the New Testament. The words about Jesus' love, compassion, and sacrifice captivated me. The more I read, the more God poured His hydration straight into my dry well.

And slowly but surely, God began that hydration process in my soul that has never stopped flowing.

What Is the Bible . . . *Really?*

Most Americans, whether Christian or not, have heard of and have even read part of the Bible. It's one of the most referenced books in our culture. Our country's forefathers based our Constitution and Declaration of Independence on values derived directly from Scripture.

In its most basic definition, the Bible is a diverse collection of inspired writings divided into two main sections:

1. The Old Testament, which tells the story of God's relationship with and work on behalf of the Hebrew people; and

2. The New Testament, which shares the story of Jesus, God's Son, and His teachings, death and resurrection, as well as the experiences and faith of the first disciples.

All Scripture was given through the inspiration of the Holy Spirit. Therefore, although it was physically written by men, God is the true author of every word of the Bible. That said, Christians hold Scripture to be without mistake.

A pastor friend recently offered an excellent analogy. He said that how we approach Scripture makes a huge difference. Either we can believe Scripture is a biography written by second-hand persons telling man-made stories, or an autobiography where God reveals Himself and our part in His story to the world.

It's similar to how teens may view a note from their parents when they plan to be out of town. They can view their parents' note simply as a list of what to do and what not to do. Or they can view it as a love letter intended to protect and guide them.

How do you view Scripture? As a set of rules or as a love letter?

Regardless of what we may tell others, we all approach Scripture with preconceptions. Our life experiences play an integral part. I grew up in a home where my parents believed in God and saw the Bible as truth from Him, even if they didn't go to church every Sunday.

Consequently, when I finally began reading Scripture for myself at age twenty-three, I approached it through these childhood filters: God is real and Scripture is how He tells us about Himself and how we are to live.

But what if your filters are different?

When I began final edits to this section of the book, I called Susan, a very dear, close friend, to gain fresh insight. Susan is an incredibly smart woman and one of the most literate, well-read people in my circle of friends.

She's also an atheist.

Since we've been friends for almost twenty years, she wasn't offended in the least to share her perspective and answer some difficult questions. May I say something here? We ALL need friends like Susan. We can learn so much from each other and broaden our scope of understanding.

Since I assumed she had never read the Bible, I asked her if it was because she didn't believe the Bible was true.

My question proved once again how I should never assume anything, because her response absolutely floored me.

Susan revealed that she has actually read the Bible from cover to cover. She's also read the Koran, the teachings of Buddha, and many other religious writings. She followed the discovery and revelation of the Dead Sea Scrolls with great interest.

She believes it's important for everyone to read the Bible and those other particular religious teachings because they represent important literary works that provide cultural insight and some historical accounts.

She said that if she were to suggest reading the Bible to someone, she would tell him or her to start with the New Testament. She found the Old Testament confusing and laborious with all of the "begat" language. (I agree with her completely on this point, by the way.)

Susan admits to finding grains of truth in various biblical stories and accounts. She cited Noah and the ark as an example. Archaeological science has proven that massive floods occurred in antiquity. She has viewed documentaries about the remains of an ark-type structure on Mount Ararat. With that evidence at hand, she believes the Bible likely contains some fact regarding the flood.

However, she doesn't believe God instructed Noah to build an ark to save humankind from being obliterated from the face of the earth.

Although her mother took her to church on occasion when she was a young girl, Susan admits that she's never believed that

God exists or that the Bible contains writings inspired by God. She views the Bible as a collection of stories written by men through the centuries.

Consequently, since she has never believed God exists, she approached reading Scripture through the filter of atheism.

She concluded by saying, "I read it because it's the most important work ever written. I just don't think you can be well rounded if you've never informed yourself of something as important as the world's religions."

Do you know anyone who holds a similar view?

Do you?

Approaching Scripture for serious study needs to originate from an openness and a desire for transformation.

Looking back, I initially studied Scripture for the wrong reason. I read it with the intent to show off by reciting passages to the Church People. It was like passing a bird feeder filled with seeds. I would read part of Scripture and pass it straight on to someone else for show without allowing God the time to sow those seeds in my life so they could take root.

I thought that if I could prove that I knew what the Bible contained, I would be part of the club. In truth, a vibrant relationship with Jesus has nothing to do with what others perceive. It has everything to do with allowing His life-giving truths to transform our lives.

Allowing God unfettered access to our heart and mind when we seek Him through His Word brings about transformation:

> Do not conform to the pattern of this world, but
> be transformed by the renewing of your mind.
> Then you will be able to test and approve what
> God's will is—His good, pleasing and perfect
> will. Romans 12:2 (NIV)

Renewal of our minds occurs when we spend time in God's transforming Word. You may get frustrated along the journey, but instead of giving up and putting aside the Bible for good, pause. Take a deep breath. Pray. Ask God for understanding. It may be years before God clarifies certain passages in our mind. Trust His timing. He will provide insight when He knows we are ready to receive it.

If you're a parent, think of it this way: You would never consider giving your six-year-old a copy of *The Canterbury Tales* by Chaucer. As a mature adult, you understand there are many years of growth and maturity required before your child is ready for such a literary work.

God, our Father, knows that new Christians need time to mature spiritually. Learn the basics. For that reason, it's a good idea to start reading at the Gospels instead of the Old Testament (like Susan suggested). The Gospels recount the inspired witness to Jesus that reveals His divinity, His moral teaching, and His sacrifice to save us from death.

There are many reasons to read Scripture, but the primary reason is that at its core, the Bible points to Jesus Christ and what He accomplished for us. Jesus said, "These are the very Scriptures that testify about Me" (John 5:39, NIV). The Bible reveals the Good News of God's relentless pursuit to reconcile us to Himself.

In other words, the Bible confirms just how much God loves us, and how He inspired men to record every word of Scripture:

> All Scripture is God-breathed and is useful for teaching, rebuking, correcting and training in righteousness. 2 Timothy 3:16 (NIV)

The Bible wasn't given merely for literary sake or to keep Christians occupied and out of trouble. We're not saved because a Bible sits on our coffee table. We're saved because Jesus, brought to light in those inspired words, provides the hope of salvation to all.

Rightly interpreting Scripture is based on having a right view of God. That holds true for many things of life. Interpreting a schematic correctly, for example, is dependent on having a right view of mathematics and engineering.

The right view of who God is, how He operates, and the nature of His character is found in Jesus. Jesus is "the image of the invisible God" (Colossians 1:15) and "the exact imprint of His nature" (Hebrews 1:3). If you want to know what God is like, then look no further than Jesus.

We come to know Jesus through studying Scripture. Studying the Bible isn't about how much we can recite; it's about how much we can learn. The more time we spend in Scripture, the more we know what our heavenly Father reveals there and the more we allow God to transform our lives through the power of those words. As He continuously transforms us, we live out His love to the world, which is critical in reaching the lost.

Our faith and living an authentic life of Christian love will be the only Bible that some people ever see. Our job is to love people like Jesus did, but unless we devote intentional time to the study of God's Word, we won't know how to do that.

I cherish Susan. But I cannot make her believe that God exists. That job belongs exclusively to the Holy Spirit. What I can do is demonstrate an authentic faith in my daily life. I can be sure not to do or say anything that poses a stumbling block for her.

And I can love Susan like Jesus does.

Sometimes the faith life you and I live is the only way some people will see how much God loves them.

I don't know about you, but for me, that sheds a completely different light on the importance of studying Scripture!

Grace and Truth

As a new Christian, perhaps you believe the path you've walked is unredeemable. You remember all the bad things you've said and done. Perhaps you've even cursed God for the heartbreaks and heartaches in your life.

God already knows where we've walked and how we've talked. God could strike us down this very moment for being horrible sinners. God has the right to pulverize me into hourglass sand for my willful stupidity.

That's the truth. But God isn't just a God of truth:

> And the Word became flesh and dwelt among us, and we have seen His glory, glory as of the only Son from the Father, full of grace and truth. John 1:14

God is full of truth AND grace. Grace is God's unmerited favor. It's a kindness from God we don't deserve. There's nothing we have done, nor can ever do, to earn this favor.

It is a gift from God. We didn't pay for that gift. His Son did.

When we sin and mess up, God extends grace instead of punishment.

Love instead of withdrawal.

Kindness instead of judgment.

God puts an *and* where our shame wants to put an *or*. Grace AND truth.

Some people may believe God is all about grace. Well, God is all grace, but He is also bigger than grace. He's also full of truth. He's not half and half. He's whole and whole. All grace and all truth. When we understand that, we realize that God is not like us. He is fully God and fully man. He's big enough to be both.

At the other end of the spectrum, some people are so serious about proclaiming the truth that they don't include God's grace. The truth is that we are so full of sin that we deserve hell. Period.

Conveying the truth of God's Word about sin is important, but Jesus never said we should use it to bludgeon people.

Truth without love convicts and condemns.

Grace cushions and absolves.

Grace proclaims that even despite what we deserve, "God

shows His love for us in that while we were still sinners, Christ died for us" (Romans 5:8).

God's truth and grace are not an either/or proposition. Although God knows our complete history—thoughts, words, and deeds—He still loves us beyond our wildest imagination. Understanding God's grace and truth is why it's important to keep reading Scripture, especially Jesus' life and ministry in the Gospels.

Let's pose a relatable scenario. If you're a mom or dad, how much do you love your child? Does that level of love for your child change when he messes up? talks back? wrecks the car? You may be mad or hurt, but you still love him and would sacrifice much for him.

That provides a tiny glimpse at how much God loves us. How can I be so sure? *Because the Bible tells me so.*

(You saw that one coming, right?)

None of the rules of Christianity make sense if we don't first understand the grace of Christ.

Spending time in Scripture reveals God's passionate pursuit of every single person who has ever lived. Through it, He invites us to enter into a personal relationship with Him.

God Has a Plan

Since He created us, God knows the best plan for our life to operate at maximum potential. Similar to a loving mother or father, God set boundaries for His children to protect and guide our lives. His plans aren't laid out in rules just to make life difficult, though many believe that is the case.

Reading Scripture brings to light His plans:

> "For I know the plans I have for you," declares the LORD, "plans to prosper you and not to harm you, plans to give you hope and a future." Jeremiah 29:11 (NIV)

His plans are meant to save us for eternity prosper us, not oppress and suffocate. It took many years of God patiently working through my stubbornness for me to understand that truth. I saw Christianity as a list of onerous rules made up by the Church People to take the fun out of life. Like a toddler relegated to time-out.

Nothing could have been further from the truth.

Scripture reveals the greatest love story ever told. As a card-carrying romantic, that makes my heart go pitter-patter. Regardless of who does or does not love me on earth, the One who created me loves me immeasurably.

The Bible chronicles God's loving pursuit of us to be in relationship with Him. He provided a beautiful nursery called earth and a beautiful eternal home called heaven. And in His great love, He sent His Son as a sacrifice, which opens the path home for all.

Scripture reveals how easy it would be for God to wipe the earth clean and start over. But His love and grace are so great that He spares us time and time again. The Bible's focus isn't on the rules. It's on God's matchless love and priceless grace.

Jesus affirmed the importance and authority of Scripture:

> Man shall not live by bread alone, but by
> every word that comes from the mouth of God.
> Matthew 4:4

To know Scripture generally is to know God vaguely. In today's world where promises easily break, Scripture showcases our Promise Keeper, who maintains an unbreakable track record of faithfulness.

If we desire to develop a relationship with someone, we intentionally spend time with him or her. We come to understand God, Jesus, and the work of the Holy Spirit by spending time with them in the pages of the Bible. There, God reveals Himself to us and patiently draws us into that relationship.

The Teachings of Jesus

The Bible records some hard-to-grasp teachings of Jesus during His three years of public ministry. His shocking and controversial words directly opposed the culture of that day. He made statements such as:

> You have heard that it was said, "You shall love your neighbor and hate your enemy." But I say to you, Love your enemies and pray for those who persecute you. Matthew 5:43–44

> You have heard that it was said, "An eye for an eye and a tooth for a tooth." But I say to you, Do not resist the one who is evil. But if anyone slaps you on the right cheek, turn to him the other also. Matthew 5:38–39

In both of these passages, Jesus first points out the world's viewpoint about how to treat people. Then He deflates our tendencies toward self-centeredness and revenge by urging us to love others, forgive hurts, and extend grace.

Not in our strength, but in His.

Jesus told people truths that they didn't want to hear. The people hated the Romans and their oppressive taxes, but Jesus told them to respect the authority of their leaders and pay their taxes. His statements like these did not win Him any popularity contests.

But Jesus didn't come to be popular. He came to save us from hell.

Sometimes the things in Scripture seem outlandish or even hard to believe. What about God parting the Red Sea, or Noah and the flood? Modern archeological advances in technology and science support those biblical narratives and countless others. For instance, chariot wheels have been discovered at the bottom of the Red Sea. One of the explorers said, "Cameras mounted on remote-controlled submarines revealed coral-encrusted chariot parts, horse and human remains strewn like battlefield wreckage on the bottom of the reed sea."[5] (The term "reed sea" is the literal translation of the words *yam suph* in Scripture, referring to the body of water that God miraculously opened so the ancient Israelites could cross on dry land before God allowed the waters to rush back, drowning the Egyptians who were in hot pursuit.)

Although Scripture provides accurate, historical accounts, it serves a higher purpose. God expands and grows our faith as we study His Word:

> Consequently, faith comes from hearing the message, and the message is heard through the word of Christ. Romans 10:17 (NIV)

When we read the message, we hear the saving message of Christ.

God's Words for God's People

As a new Christian, it was incredibly difficult for me to set aside presuppositions, worldviews, and existing beliefs. We've been given one Bible, but there are millions of other books that present opposite viewpoints. Yet none of them can claim to be the inspired Word of God Almighty.

Faith comes down to believing God and trusting that He wants only the best for His children.

Let's look at Noah and the ark, since we've already touched on that story. I realize that using Noah as an example of faith and trust may seem odd, since he didn't study a Bible for guidance. It didn't exist then as we know it today.

However, Genesis 6:8 reveals: "But Noah found favor in the eyes of the LORD." In other words, Noah knew God. That's faith. And he trusted God's guidance. To go a step further, Noah didn't need a Bible because he received instructions from God Himself:

> And God said to Noah, "I have determined to make an end of all flesh, for the earth is

filled with violence through them. Behold, I will destroy them with the earth. Make yourself an ark of gopher wood. Make rooms in the ark, and cover it inside and out with pitch. This is how you are to make it: the length of the ark 300 cubits, its breadth 50 cubits, and its height 30 cubits. Make a roof for the ark, and finish it to a cubit above, and set the door of the ark in its side. Make it with lower, second, and third decks. For behold, I will bring a flood of waters upon the earth to destroy all flesh in which is the breath of life under heaven. Everything that is on the earth shall die." Genesis 6:13–17

God's instructions seem like an odd request to us even today, but they were more so for Noah. Noah lived in a desert climate where rain had never fallen. And an ark? I wonder if Noah even had a clue about what one looked like. It would be similar to someone telling you that jieuzth would be falling from the sky and you would need a giebonfu to survive. Nonsensical, right?

Despite his lack of understanding, Noah trusted the Instructor:

Noah was a righteous man, blameless in his generation. Noah walked with God. Genesis 6:9

Noah knew his heavenly Father because he walked with Him. In other words, he spent time with God. Noah relied on God's promises to provide for those who love Him and obey His commandments.

So he built an ark.

Noah received these instructions from God at the young, strapping age of five hundred. By the time he finished the ark, he was six hundred. It took Noah a hundred years—a century!—to build the ark. We can almost hear one hundred years of his neighbors questioning his sanity, most making fun of him for building something so strange for a purpose they did not understand or care about.

Perhaps when you tell others the ways you follow God, they may mock you or make fun of you. Every Christian who lives his or her faith openly experiences such responses from people who do not understand the big picture.

Noah worked with single-minded tenacity. He may have been scared. After all, God told him that everything on earth would die. He may have doubted. After all, he was old and didn't know how much time he had left on earth. He may have questioned. After all, who was he that God should choose him and his family to survive the pending doomsday?

He followed the word of God from God Himself. Although he did not understand the big picture at the time, Noah trusted God.

Noah could not see what life would hold beyond the flood. Perhaps he could not imagine never again seeing his extended family and friends, his home and community. God did not provide a timeline for how long Noah would remain on the ark. God never promised that Noah would even see dry land again. All Noah knew was that he would spend an unspecified amount of time on an ark with seven family members and countless pairs of animals that probably didn't smell good.

Still, Noah trusted God.

You and I can develop deeper trust as we read through Scripture and walk with God as well. Although we do not hear God audibly, we have the privilege of following God's Word, inspired by God Himself, of hearing the Gospel proclaimed in the worship service. If we want to survive and thrive, then knowing God and trusting His plans makes all the difference. Ralph Waldo Emerson once said, "All I have seen teaches me to trust the Creator for all I have not seen."

Exactly.

God did not provide vague instructions to Noah. He provided exact measurements for how to build the ark, down to the last cubit. God was about to send the mother of all storms upon the earth, so He provided Noah the faith and knowledge required to survive.

Put that in context with your life. One day you will breathe your last. As an eternal being, your soul will spend eternity in either heaven or hell. God provides Scripture for the knowledge through faith required to survive: "Whoever believes in Him should not perish but have eternal life" (John 3:16).

God watches over and protects His children. His constant vision is our constant provision.

Five "Texts" That Compete with Scripture

Modern technology provides plentiful access to sermon podcasts and live-streaming Christian events, as well as a plethora of study guides and resources to further our understanding of Scripture.

However, these things can never replace spending time in Scripture itself.

The Reformers cried, "*Sola Scriptura!*" which is Latin for "Scripture alone!" By that proclamation, they placed the Bible firmly at the top of the stack when it came to ways Christians obtain truth. Scripture has the final say.

When the apostle Paul and Silas (a spiritual leader or overseer in the assembly of believers at Jerusalem) arrived in the town called Berea, here's what happened:

> The brothers immediately sent Paul and Silas away by night to Berea, and when they arrived they went into the Jewish synagogue. Now these Jews were more noble than those in Thessalonica; they received the word with all eagerness, examining the Scriptures daily to see if these things were so. Many of them therefore believed, with not a few Greek women of high standing as well as men. Acts 17:10–12

The Berean Jews were "more noble" because of their willing reception of the Word of God. Unlike the Thessalonian Jews, they were eager to hear the teaching of Paul and Silas.

Bereans spent time "examining the Scriptures" daily to evaluate the truth of various teachings. Oh, that God would increase the tribe of Bereans in the Church today! With the cacophony of other "texts" clamoring for our fidelity, taking time to compare what we hear to Scripture proves vital.

⁓The Text of Emotions

"Follow your heart. Trust your heart. What are your emotions telling you?" As a woman, I'm the last person to throw cold water on the flames of emotion. But can we agree they are a fickle and erratic guide for life?

If we based our life on how we feel, we'd never work full time, no marriage would last past the first bump, and kids would be given to gypsies in eight days.

If emotions provided our ultimate guide, we'd be easy prey for manipulative preachers, persuasive panhandlers, and calculating politicians.

Emotions can deceive us. Today's compelling feeling is product for tomorrow's regret. Chances are you already know that. Yes, there is truth in the text of emotions, but it cannot be the final, binding truth.

When emotions speak, spend time examining the Scriptures daily to see if these things are so.

⁓The Text of Experience

The opportunity knocked at just the right time, the money miraculously appeared, and your Mr. McDreamy showed up on the doorstep unexpectedly. Are they signs from God? Definitely maybe.

Remember Moses in front of Pharaoh? God turned Moses' staff into a serpent, but the magicians of Egypt had magic of their own. Then what? When you see an infomercial inviting you to a lifelong quest to see the world on the same day you received your brand-new passport, do you get to turn to your spouse and announce, "Honey, let's pack our bags and sell the house"?

Maybe. But only after you spend time examining the Scriptures daily to see if these things are so.

◠ The Text of the Voice of Angels and God

"God told me," she said. And she followed that voice to pray with someone who she did not know was contemplating suicide. *That's cool*, I think. *But what about this . . .*

"God told me," she said. And she followed that voice to marry an abuser who wrecked her life and damaged their children. And what about this . . .

"God told me," he said. And he followed that voice to train pilots to fly planes into high-rise buildings.

For every "God told me" story that ends well, I can tell you that there many that don't. They ended in financial ruin, hope melted, and hearts shattered.

Besides, once you fling "God told me" into a discussion, who can argue? Right or wrong, the opposition appears anti-God. Paul counseled:

> But even if we or an angel from heaven should preach to you a gospel contrary to the one we preached to you, let him be accursed.
> Galatians 1:8

Yes, through the Holy Spirit, God guides our path. But before you follow the voice you thought you heard, spend time examining the Scriptures daily to see if these things are so.

⌒ The Text of Preachers and Popes

"God told me to tell you to plant a seed of faith in my ministry, so get out that credit card and plant a big one." Ugh. God never called His people to be mindless followers of preachers and popes. When the APOSTLE Paul taught the Bereans, they didn't just swallow his teachings. "Unroll the scrolls!" they cried. "Because this man's teaching is subject to Scripture, and not the other way around."

Sola Scriptura!

When Martin Luther discovered widespread misunderstanding and corruption in the Roman Catholic Church, he nailed a piece of parchment to the Castle Church in Wittenberg, Germany, containing the ninety-five revolutionary opinions that would begin the Protestant Reformation. He declared at the resulting trial:

> Unless I am convinced by the testimony of the Holy Scriptures or by evident reason—for I can believe neither pope nor councils alone, as it is clear that they have erred repeatedly and contradicted themselves—I consider myself convicted by the testimony of Holy Scripture, which is my basis; my conscience is captive to the Word of God. Thus I cannot and will not recant, because acting against one's conscience is neither safe nor sound. God help me. Amen.

Because no matter what the preacher or pope says, it is the duty and privilege of all God's saints to spend time examining the Scriptures daily to see if these things are so.

⌒ The Text of Self-Will

Here we come to the most prevalent and widely accepted opponent to the authority of the Bible: our self-gratification-addicted culture that bellows, "I want to do what I want to do. I know what's best for me. Period." "No one can tell me what to do! Your truth isn't my truth!" "I believe that what's right for me isn't right for other people. Anything goes as long as no harm is done."

Listen. There is a truth that roars louder—Christ's voice is Scripture's voice.

Yet we would rather read the text of our own agendas and self-governance any day. Some people pick and choose from every other text, every other discipline, to assemble a self-made truth system, like selecting from fruits and vegetables at a farmer's market.

People who do this become their own god.

Having spent time in my early Christian years doing that very thing, I can tell you that never works out well. Ever.

The bottom line is that these various other texts might speak grains of truth, but all texts are inferior to the sacred text of Scripture because they don't come from the one true God.

If you want to know if you are leading a God-pleasing life and accomplishing the purposes for which He created us, then read what God says to you in His Word. Spending daily time in Scripture is imperative.

Crucial to life.

Critical to hope.

Central to love.

A PAUSE AT THE WELL

Let's take a moment to pause for some practical application.

1. We spent some time looking at various texts that compete with Scripture in our culture. Did you identify with any of them as an area where you struggle?

2. Despite not knowing what God's plans were for the ark, Noah trusted and obeyed God, even when it didn't make sense. Do you have any areas in your life where you are holding back from trusting God and following His instructions?

3. Have you ever read the Bible from cover to cover? And if so, has it been a long time since you did so? Romans 10:17 reminds us that "faith comes from hearing the message, and the message is heard through the word of Christ" (NIV).

The benefits of reading Scripture daily compose a list too long to enumerate here. If you have never read through the Bible or if it has been a long time, find a reading plan that fits your schedule and dive in.

- -

PRAYER STARTER

Take some time to identify areas in your life where it is a challenge for you to trust God and follow His instructions. One by one, ask God to reveal the reason and emotion behind each of these challenges, and then surrender it to Him, asking Him to strengthen your faith toward obedience.

- -

PART II

VETERAN DISCIPLES OF JESUS

Human nature is like water.
It takes the shape of its container.

Wallace Stevens

Life in us is like the water in a river.

Henry David Thoreau

CHAPTER 7

FAITH OVERBOARD, WITH A SPLASH OF CRAZY

But when he saw the wind, he was afraid, and beginning to sink he cried out, "Lord, save me." Jesus immediately reached out His hand and took hold of him, saying to him, "O you of little faith, why did you doubt?"

~ Matthew 14:30–31

It was a tiny step of faith. Noticeable to no one else but me. And perhaps one other.

For eight months, I had been attending church with the gentleman who had initially invited me. But I made the drive only if he met me in the church parking lot. He served as my buffer. Although they went out of their way to be nice, the Church People still intimidated me.

We had recently begun attending Bible class together. Naturally, I had spent time familiarizing myself with locating the books in the Bible. I didn't want to look stupid. Actually learning what each book contained wasn't as important to me at the time. Outward appearances still sat at the top of my list.

We chose a Bible class led by one of the pastors. He was a gifted teacher who made the stories come to life. He incorporated relevant, life-application principles that applied to everyday life. For the first time, I heard about God's love and grace in a way that I could understand.

I was hooked.

Then, early one Sunday, as I was just rubbing the sleep from my eyes, my boyfriend called to say he was sick and couldn't meet me at church. After promising to take homemade soup to him later, I grabbed my purse, keys, and Bible and headed out the door to church.

Halfway to church, two revelations hit me: (1) I would be walking into church by myself for the very first time, and (2) it hadn't occurred to me to stay home.

Going to church had become ingrained much more deeply than I realized. It wasn't just going to church that made the difference. It was the Church People. Their circle of love expanded to absorb me. Welcomed me with open arms. Loved me despite my hesitation.

That morning's drive was a tiny step. But it was HUGE.

Now, twenty-three years later, I cannot imagine Sunday without church.

Life without faith.

Facing death without Christ.

God has enriched and blessed my life beyond measure with vibrant, Christ-centered friendships.

As a "veteran" Christian, I now have the joyful privilege of welcoming the timid, mentoring the lost, and teaching God's truths. I could not have possibly imagined this path of faith, but now I cannot imagine anything else.

This journey is no longer about feeling safe and secure in my faith. It's about living that faith out loud—even in the midst of failure.

And there have been plenty of those.

By God's grace, I'm now drinking from the well that gives me "living water."

Risky Faith

When it comes to impetuous, live-on-the-edge faith, Peter automatically comes to mind. Poor Peter. Time and again, he leaped into action without thinking through potential adverse results.

Near the end of Jesus' earthly ministry, Peter tried to prevent Jesus from going into Jerusalem, fearing for Jesus' life. Jesus called him Satan. Ouch.

Peter stepped out of a boat in the middle of a terrible storm because he wanted to be out there with Jesus, walking on the water. He took six steps, became fearful, and cried out. Jesus reached out to save him and told Peter that he had a doubting faith. Ouch again.

But Peter was not afraid to jump. Isn't that what's behind the heart of faith?

Bravery is contagious.

So is timidity.

How shall we live as veteran followers of Christ? Let's take the lead from Peter's life. You've heard the story of Peter faithfully stepping out of the boat many times. You have likely taught it and could recite it by heart.

But it's what happened when Peter got back in the boat that hit me hardest just a few short months ago. At this point in my discipleship journey, it spoke to me through the megaphone of humility, forgiveness, and leadership.

Faith: Taking a Leap or Taking a Seat?

Jesus had just finished feeding thousands with five loaves and two fish (Matthew 14:13–21). It was an epic, jaw-dropping miracle. When the long day was over, Jesus sent the disciples in a boat across the Sea of Galilee while He dismissed the crowd.

The disciples weighed anchor, Jesus dismissed the crowd, and then He went up the mountainside to spend a long time with His Father in prayer.

By the time Jesus had finished praying, it was the middle of the night. The disciples were still in the boat and had encountered a terrible storm as they attempted to cross the Sea of Galilee. The wind and waves threatened disaster. Here's how the story goes:

> When evening came, He was there alone, but the boat by this time was a long way from the land, beaten by the waves, for the wind was against them. And in the fourth watch of the night He came to them, walking on the sea. But when the disciples saw Him walking on the sea, they were terrified, and said, "It is a ghost!" and they cried out in fear. But immediately Jesus spoke to them, saying, "Take heart; it is I. Do not be afraid." And Peter answered Him, "Lord, if it is You, command me to come to You on the water." He said, "Come." So Peter got out of the boat and walked on the water and came to Jesus. Matthew 14:23–29

True to form, Peter is the first to react. He's the first to test the waters of faith. Peter wasn't afraid. Not because he was an experienced fisherman who knew how to handle a boat. But because he heard Jesus' words of assurance. He may not have recognized Jesus through the storm's debris, but he knew his Savior's voice.

When the storms of life hit, we'll find ourselves in serious trouble if we cannot recognize Jesus' voice above the world's noise. His melody in the storm's dissonance. His calm above chaotic circumstances.

Now, I've never heard Jesus actually talking, but I've come to recognize Jesus' voice through His words in Scripture: "Whoever is of God hears the words of God" (John 8:47).

When difficulties rear and the enemy roars, God provides us with specific words for particular situations. It's the Greek word *rhema* that comes into play. A *rhema* is a verse or portion of Scripture that the Holy Spirit brings to our attention with application to a current situation or need for direction:

> But He *answered*, "It is written, 'Man shall not
> live by bread alone, but by every word that
> comes from the mouth of God.'" Matthew 4:4
> (emphasis added)

Hearing the *rhema* of God comes from daily reading God's *logos* (the entirety of His words, the Bible).

The storms of life continue to strike throughout our journey of faith. We need His words of hope and assurance. And remember, we're not exempt from the storms just because we follow Christ. Neither were Peter and the other disciples in that storm-tossed boat.

But the good news is that although life's storms will drench us, God's living water still hydrates us from the inside out. Some may shake their heads at Peter's seemingly rash behavior. But at least he got out of the boat. He may have been afraid, but he heard the Lord's urging and followed.

Leaping takes great faith.

The other eleven disciples sat back on their spiritual haunches and stayed put. They chose to watch to see if Peter would fail.

The Church today is full of similar pew sitters. They watch as others take a leap of faith with a new ministry initiative or mission project, waiting to see what will happen. They wonder: "Will they take a nosedive?"

Pew sitters are the first to criticize and the last to volunteer. Such behavior reflects a parched life, devoid of God's hydration. They are the first to speak and the last to act, and they offer plenty of suggestions on how the church needs to run. But when it's time to engage and actually do the work, they hide behind the badge of busyness.

Sound familiar?

Like Peter, the other eleven disciples had walked with Jesus. They had seen Jesus heal the sick, raise the dead, cast out demons, and perform many other miracles. They had heard His words and eaten fish with the thousands just a few hours earlier. So why didn't they have the faith to take the leap with Peter?

Perhaps they were too busy calculating their chance of survival.

Their own strength.

What involvement might cost them.

By weighing the pros and cons, their inaction whispered fear into Peter's determination. We find that true in our friendships as well. Our friends may not say that they don't agree with what we're doing, but their choice not to engage speaks loud and clear. It may cause us to doubt or fear what we're doing.

As Christ followers, we will encounter those who admonish us to stay in the boat. But we are ultimately accountable to the One who equipped us, not to those who threaten us with the "what if's."

We can only imagine the disciples' reaction when they realize Peter's intent to abandon ship. And while they fret, Peter is already overboard:

> So Peter got out of the boat and walked on the
> water and came to Jesus. But when he saw the
> wind, he was afraid, and beginning to sink he
> cried out, "Lord, save me." Jesus immediately
> reached out His hand and took hold of him,
> saying to him, "O you of little faith, why did
> you doubt?" Matthew 14: 29–31

I don't know about you, but when I first read this story in Scripture, it bothered me what Jesus said to Peter: "O you of little faith, why did you doubt?" I mean, in the realm of faith, weren't there eleven bigger failures still sitting in the boat? At least Peter had the faith to step out!

But that's not the point.

The point is that Peter doubted Jesus.

Peter shouted out his doubt directly to Jesus: "Lord, save me."

Jesus didn't ridicule Peter for stepping out in faith. He was admonishing Peter for doubting. For taking his eyes off Jesus to notice the wind. For allowing fear to prevail.

Peter, with his risk-taking faith, gained experiential knowledge that the other disciples did not. He met Jesus face-to-face. When he began to sink, he felt Jesus' hand pull him out of danger. In that life-altering, faith-confirming moment, Peter knew beyond the shadow of a doubt that Jesus could save him.

The others observed it.

But Peter experienced it.

We don't know we can walk on water until we follow the Water Walker into the waves. Benjamin Franklin said, "Tell me and I forget, teach me and I may remember, involve me and I learn." Teaching others about faith only conveys information.

Faith by active involvement opens the door to transformational learning. That is a cornerstone of hydrated living.

If we never take leaps of faith and allow Jesus to rescue us from life's storms, then we only pass along our faith through observations instead of first-hand, life-changing experiences. Risk-taking faith triumphs over scientific surveillance when it comes to our spiritual growth.

It's important to note that Peter stepped out of the boat only after receiving confirmation that it was Jesus doing the calling: "Lord, if it's You . . . ."

We can leap into all kinds of things, but unless we've received confirmation from the Lord to jump, we are leaping into the deep end by ourselves. Following our own agenda can harm us and everyone else in the boat with us.

God orchestrates opportunities for us to step out.

I could have chosen to stay home the day my boyfriend was sick, but I would have never experienced the personal love and acceptance from the Church People. My leap looked like getting into my car. Although I never intentionally sought it, attending church alone that day was a gigantic leap of faith. I went by myself, but did not find myself alone when I arrived. I was welcomed with open arms, without reservation, into the fold. No hesitation or reservation.

God's wellspring of life never fails to strengthen us for the journey ahead.

That was the day that I knew I was accepted as ME. Not because I was their friend's girlfriend. In my mind, that translated directly to my relationship with God.

Since His people accepted me, so would He.

That day, the faith that God had called me toward became mine.

Faith Strengthened through Failure

But what about those times when we take leaps and the storm overwhelms us? Peter leapt. And sunk. Even with his Savior right before his eyes.

When we fail, we don't feel like poster children for Christianity. Through faith, Jesus is ever before us, so why do we tend to focus on our sinking fiasco instead of His saving grace? Because we're human.

In truth, even our failures point us to the One who can repair our broken pieces.

My failure: I'm divorced. Regardless of fault, my marriage failed. That makes me half a failure. I could choose to let that failure define me. Instead, I choose to allow God to redeem it for His purposes and glory. God has used that failure to open countless doors for me to pass along experiential principles of forgiveness that He taught me in that storm.

Failure is the litmus test of faith.

The gauge for our well's depth.

The pinch test for hydration.

In that steadfast striving comes the saving of our faith. The resolve to continue listening, leaping, and reaching provides our faith room to grow.

Faith is strengthened in the storms, but it is sustained in God's wellspring of life. Always believe Him beyond what you can see.

Failure is just part of the faith-refining process.

The Two-Step of Risky Faith

As veteran Christians, I pray that we boldly step into those leaps of faith.

Our senses rebel when we move forward to step but can't see the ground. Or the safety net. Or the outcome. Acrophobics suffer nightmares from such scenarios. It's like riding in the front car of a roller coaster. The scariest part is when it reaches the top of the incline and we can't see the tracks. Fear and doubt cause us to scream as the plummet begins.

We may not be able to see the tracks, but they're there. We may not be able to see Jesus physically, but He is ever present.

Eyesight has very little to do with faith. In fact, Scripture explicitly states, "For we walk by faith, not by sight" (2 Corinthians 5:7).

Such teaching grates against modern thinking. Intellectuals purport uncertain steps as foolishness in the extreme. Stepping where the ground is unclear doesn't earn the popular vote. Yet what the world belittles as illogical, Jesus honors as faith.

Jesus wasn't determined to win a popularity contest. He was determined to win our souls for eternity.

Taking a step of faith is actually a two-step process. Or dance, if you will. Just picture Peter stepping out of the boat. The first step happens when he decides to swing his leg overboard and get his toes wet. But he can still choose to pull his leg back into the boat. He hasn't totally committed.

The second step involves shifting his weight and hoisting the rest of his body overboard. Once the second step is under way, there's no turning back. We will either walk on water (so to speak) or sink.

Peter's step of faith was riskier than we give him credit for. It wasn't just the fear of stepping out. The boat carrying Peter and the other eleven disciples was being beaten and tossed by a violent night-time storm. Peter stepped out of the boat at the most dangerous time possible.

Sometimes I have trouble stepping out in faith when there's not a storm cloud of doubt in sight. But impetuous, live-life-on-the-edge, all-or-nothing Peter wanted to make sure Jesus would be there for him, even in the storm.

What a hydrated testimony of walking by faith!

Peter needed assurance that it was Jesus who appeared inside the storm: "Lord, if it is You, command me to come to You on the water." Jesus invited Peter, so over the side he went.

Peter had no clue how that scene would conclude, but by trusting and performing the faith two-step, he learned firsthand that Jesus is stronger than any storm.

Peter bravely faced the waves. The other disciples just, well ... waved.

Waved at Peter as he left.

Waved at Jesus when He called.

And Jesus had no words for the disciples who remained in the boat. They were mere observers instead of active participants. Observers tend to have selective hearing, but Jesus' actions spoke loud and clear.

Walking by faith and not by sight means moving past simply waving at Jesus to actually following Him. Exercising faith means treading into the unknown or uncertain. We cannot discover the unknown without consenting to lose sight of what is known.

Christians need to stop living as if our purpose is to arrive safely at death.

I once believed that it was reckless to take a leap of faith out of a perfectly good boat. Out of my comfort zone. My preset view of life. But over time, God's relentless, loving pursuit after me and His hydrating words provided the assurance I needed to become a brave believer.

Because experience has taught me that Jesus waits on the waves.

Faith Worships Wet

The problem with doing the faith two-step out of the boat is that we'll get wet. Now, as a native Texas girl with a southern poof, I naturally think of my hair first. I know . . . shallow, right?

In Peter's case, between the storm and sinking in the water, he got soaked to the skin. Although Peter's failure is well known, what immediately follows receives little press. Yet it captures one of the most important concepts for veteran Christians and leaders:

> And when they got into the boat, the wind ceased. And those in the boat worshiped Him, saying, "Truly You are the Son of God." Matthew 14:32–33

That wasn't what I would have expected. I imagined the disciples gathering around Peter to offer reassurance. Or perhaps a towel to dry off. But that isn't what happened.

Instead, they worshiped Jesus.

Did they even care that Peter almost *died*? I can easily picture poor Peter over in the corner of the boat, shivering, while the others sing, "A mighty fortress is our God, a bulwark never failing!" But evidently nobody cares that Peter almost drowned.

Interestingly enough, neither does Peter.

The old saying comes to mind: "It's not how you start, it's how you finish." Well, Peter finished by sinking. He finished all wet. We want to come to Jesus when we're dry, don't we? When life runs smoothly. When we've got all of our stuff in order. Safe on dry land and in broad daylight.

But sometimes we are submerged in sin. Soaked by failure. We don't want to come to Jesus until we dry off. That's the shame game. It's easy to believe that we have a solid relationship when the sun is out and everything in our garden is rosy. But what about when we're all wet and it's dark?

Veteran Christian, are you soaked today?

Leader, are you waterlogged today?

You and I have to learn how to worship wet. Sometimes we've got to lead, teach, and reach out when we are soaked to the bone. We love welcoming people to worship who have been wet their whole lives. They don't know God's ways. They need His salvation. So we open the door wide to let them come to Jesus.

But reality provides another camera angle.

Sometimes we aren't very graceful about allowing wet disciples to come to Jesus. You know, those good Christians who have walked the faith journey and have a pretty good grasp of Scripture who were formerly dry. But they've sunk into sin. And now they're wet.

We tend to think that those wet people should know better, right? Know better than to let sin submerge them. So instead of welcoming them back with open arms, we chide, "You don't have a lot to worship about, do you? You need to drop your hands, drop to your knees, and work your stuff out."

In other words, "Dry yourself off."

But that's never Jesus' response to us. He never expects us to solve our sins because He knows that without Him, we can't. We need time and His loving guidance to dry off. That evening wasn't about Peter's valiant attempt. Or his crazy, overboard faith.

It was all about worshiping our Savior who rescues us when we sink.

Sometimes, walking by faith means we have to worship in the moments after we have just sunk, when we're soaking wet from failure. But when we worship wet, we're trusting that the One who controls the wind and waves will never let us drown. That the One who hydrates us sacrificed His life. He's our eternal life vest. He welcomes us back into His boat of grace, reminding us:

You're Mine.

You're forgiven.

I still love you.

You're going to be okay.

When life's storms threaten to overwhelm us, God, our rock, is the mighty refuge and solid foundation that anchors us strong.

Wet or dry.

A PAUSE AT THE WELL

Let's take a moment to pause for some practical application.

1. As we looked at the account of Peter's leap of faith out of the boat, which part of his story makes the greatest impact on you? Why?

2. When Peter gets out of the boat to walk toward Jesus, the other eleven disciples remain in the boat. Have there been times when you observed someone else's faith instead of acting on yours? What was the result?

3. Exercising faith means treading into the unknown or uncertain. It also means that we may sink. Does the thought of failure intimidate you? Does it cause you to remain seated instead of engaging?

● ●

PRAYER STARTER

Take some time to identify steps of faith that you have taken in your discipleship journey and thank God for them, one by one. For those areas of life where you may have taken a seat in the stands of faith, ask God to give you the strength to engage instead of waving from the sidelines.

● ●

CHAPTER 8

TREADING VS. TRUSTING

Then they seized Him and led Him away, bringing Him into the high priest's house, and Peter was following at a distance.

~ Luke 22:54

As he skulked in the courtyard's shadows, Simon Peter's mind whirled. The past three years had changed the trajectory of his life. He wasn't the same man anymore.

Peter was a fisherman. Had been his whole life. Fishing was a successful family business, so he spent his time baiting hooks and pulling in fish, casting nets and repairing them, and maintaining the family's boats.

But one particular day, all of that changed:

> On one occasion, while the crowd was pressing in on Him to hear the word of God, He was standing by the lake of Gennesaret, and He saw two boats by the lake, but the fishermen had gone out of them and were washing their nets. Getting into one of the boats, which was Simon's, He asked him to put out a little from the land. And He sat down and taught the people from the boat. Luke 5:1–3

Peter and his partners had been fishing all night, but the fish weren't biting. They didn't haul in a single fish. So as morning broke, they headed for shore to begin the arduous task of cleaning the nets.

Then Jesus and a whole crowd of people appeared.

I've spent plenty of time over the years fishing at night. In Texas, that's the best time to catch catfish. Dad used to take my sisters and me fishing. It was his favorite pastime. They were wonderful bonding times. But I've experienced nights when not one single fish bites. The hours drag by like the clock is going backward.

On those occasions, when our time was up, I just wanted to pack up as fast as I could, get home, shower, grab a bite, and go to bed. I didn't have enough energy left for much else. I certainly never felt like being sociable. And fishing isn't even my livelihood.

Would you be delighted in a similar circumstance? Probably

not. So we can imagine that a refreshing meal and bedtime were not in Peter's future that morning either:

> And when He had finished speaking, He said
> to Simon, "Put out into the deep and let down
> your nets for a catch." Luke 5:4

Wait . . . what? I know what *my* response would have been. It could be summed up in three words: *not very nice*. But not Peter. He chose to respond differently:

> And Simon answered, "Master, we toiled all
> night and took nothing! But at Your word I will
> let down the nets." Luke 5:5

We hear Peter's disappointment at laboring so long with nothing to show for it. He knew the fish weren't biting. Yet, take note of Peter's obedience. He called Jesus "Master," and he loaded the nets back into the boat and headed out to sea.

They had met before. Peter's brother Andrew heard John the Baptist speak and told Peter that they had found the Christ (John 1:41). Peter knew that Jesus was no ordinary man to be rudely dismissed. So he obeyed and was rewarded:

> And when they had done this, they enclosed
> a large number of fish, and their nets were
> breaking. They signaled to their partners in the
> other boat to come and help them. And they
> came and filled both the boats, so that they
> began to sink. Luke 5:6–7

That same day, Peter responded to Jesus' calling to follow Him to become a fisher of men.

Fast-forward three years. Something has gone terribly wrong. Jesus has been betrayed by one of His inner circle; He has been arrested and brought in chains to the high priest's house to be tried for false testimony—an offense that invoked the death sentence.

Peter had been with Jesus through long days, crowds pressing in on every side, and he watched Jesus perform miracles too numerous to count. Feeding the five thousand. Walking on water. Healing. Casting out demons. And so many more. Those days may have seemed a distant memory as Peter stood in the outer courtyard of the high priest, waiting to hear Jesus' fate.

Have you ever experienced drastic changes in your life? Did your life turn out exactly as you planned?

Mine neither. During those wonderful fishing times, I never planned to watch my dad deteriorate and eventually succumb to cancer.

As Christ followers, how we handle life's curveballs bears witness to the world. What does our witness say? I don't know about you, but my witness for Christ has been downright disgraceful at times. Such behavior—or misbehavior, I should say—reveals a parched life pushing away God's hydrating, transforming power to try to handle things on our own.

When I launched Artesian Ministries in 2007, I threw myself into the calling God had placed in my life: to write Bible studies and teach His Word wherever He opened a door. In between, I also worked full time, volunteered at church, sang on the worship team, kept a social calendar with family and friends, and traveled quite a bit.

In short, I was exhausted.

Sometimes we get so busy working for God that we no longer work toward spending time *with* Him. Only doing *for* Him. Always pouring out. Never pausing long enough for Him to pour in. I'm so thankful to a dear friend who loved me enough to speak the truth in love. I needed to hear her kind yet stern words cautioning me to slow down before I burned out.

It's because of my experience that I can identify with Peter as he sat in the courtyard. We can only imagine what was running through His mind.

In Luke 22, the religious leaders order soldiers to arrest Jesus so that they can kill Him and put an end to His teachings and ministry. Little did they know that it was the worst idea ever to kill the Son of God, because what happened on Easter morning guaranteed that people would talk about Jesus for the rest of time.

The night had started out smoothly as Jesus and the twelve disciples celebrated the Passover in the Upper Room. After dinner they headed toward the Garden of Gethsemane, singing the Hallel as they walked.

Jesus said He needed to pray by Himself. He posted Peter, James, and John immediately outside the gate and asked them to stay alert. To pray.

They tried to do as He had asked, but exhaustion won the battle and they slept. After Jesus woke them a third time, they jolted wide awake as Roman soldiers descended to bind Jesus in chains. One of Jesus' companions (perhaps it was impetuous Peter) lunged with a sword in His defense, cutting off the high priest's servant's ear. Jesus stepped in, calmed hot tempers, and healed the servant. (Imagine what Jesus' enemies thought about that!)

As Jesus was led away, His hour of darkness approaching, Peter's response was not what we would expect from a devoted disciple:

> Then they seized Him and led Him away,
> bringing Him into the high priest's house, and
> Peter was following at a distance. Luke 22:54

Despite Jesus' suffering, Peter followed *at a distance*. What had happened to the fisherman Jesus met three years ago—to the one who was the first person to correctly identify Jesus as "the Christ, the Son of the living God" (Matthew 16:16)?

He chose to tread water instead of trust the Wellspring of Life.

When We Tread and Follow at a Distance

Peter was a follower of Christ, but that night he followed at a distance.

If you have been a Jesus follower for any length of time, chances are there have been times where you followed at a distance. Not wanting to identify with Christ. Perhaps it was too uncomfortable. Friends didn't understand. The situation became discouraging.

Like Peter, I followed at a distance.

For several years.

I treaded on surface faith because I was more worried about outward appearances than living a hydrated life. My excuse: diving into God's wellspring still seemed scary. Taking the plunge meant I would lose control. And I wasn't completely ready to hand over the reins of my heart.

In other words, I was with Jesus, but not really. I followed Jesus, but not wholeheartedly.

If times were good, I wore the Team Jesus jersey loud and proud. It's easy being a fan because we can take off the jersey when we get home. We put it back on one day a week, and as long as He wins, we're with Him. I was for Jesus as long as Jesus was doing things for me.

Peter was treading in that courtyard. He was with Jesus, but not really. He followed Jesus, but not wholeheartedly. He followed Him at a comfortable distance. When things went forward too fast, Peter backed up.

Being close to Christ costs something. It requires us to go outside of our comfort zone. Like us, Peter had to learn that through experience.

Peter had been one of Jesus' closest friends. Peter, James, and John formed Jesus' intimate inner circle. If anyone should have gotten the message, it should have been Peter.

But something changed in Peter when he hit that courtyard:

And when they had kindled a fire in the middle

of the courtyard and sat down together, Peter
sat down among them. Luke 22:55

Peter took off the Team Jesus jersey, retreated into the crowd, and took a seat in the stands. Although he came with Christ, he chose to get comfortable with everyone but Christ. He chose safety in anonymity.

Then Peter did something that he swore directly to Jesus he would never do: he outright denied knowing Him:

Then a servant girl, seeing him as he sat in the light and looking closely at him, said, "This man also was with Him." But he denied it, saying, "Woman, I do not know Him." Luke 22:56

We read that story today and believe Peter to be a liar. But I wonder . . . was he really lying? Perhaps Peter's response simply revealed the truth in his heart.

When life runs like clockwork, you and I want others to know that we know Christ. We get all puffed up with pride that we know the main player on the team, so to speak. We get to say we "know Him" as we sport our freshly pressed Team Jesus jersey.

Yet it's one thing to wear the jersey; it's another thing to wear His ring. The Church—you and I—are the Bride of Christ. Wearing His rock means we stand with Him in good times and bad. It shows the world we belong to Him. It's not about the church we belong to. It's about the Savior we belong to.

But when life heats up, suddenly we start following Jesus at a distance. But what we need to do is this: *we need to stop stalking Jesus and begin following Him.* Believe me, I know. I stalked Jesus for several years, and I was creeping us both out.

For Peter, that night had to be the worst of the worst. Denying Christ once could mean someone just caught us off guard. Denying Christ twice is questionable.

Denying Christ three times is intentional.

Treading: People Can Spot a Counterfeit

Once we spend time with Christ, we can no longer hide in the crowd. The crowd notices a difference in us. Or at least, they should. They noticed a difference in Peter. Three people identified Peter while he attempted to blend in:

> Then a servant girl, seeing him as he sat in the light and looking closely at him, said, "This man also was with Him." But he denied it, saying, "Woman, I do not know Him." Luke 22:56–57

The crowd observed that Peter was different from them. Perhaps it was the way he dressed. Churchgoers tend to dress similarly, as well. Chances are you won't see a bikini-clad woman or a shirtless man sitting in the pew. "Modest is hottest," the trendy saying goes. We like wearing the Team Jesus jersey.

Then Peter denied Jesus a second time:

> And a little later someone else saw him and said, "You also are one of them." But Peter said, "Man, I am not." Luke 22:58

Perhaps Peter spoke like Christ. We tend to emulate leaders that we admire, so even when we try to hide them, the similarities we have with people we admire have a way of sneaking out. For instance, we might speak Christian-ese. You know, say those key words that instantly alert others to our status as Christ followers—words like *redeemed*, *sanctified*, *blessed*, and *saved*. Or we use catchphrases that only Christians understand: "Be in the world but not of the world." Trust me, non-Christians and those new to the faith do not understand phrases like that.

Although meaningful to us, the unchurched hear only the droning voice of Charlie Brown's teacher in the background: "Wah, wah, wah, wah, wah, wah." It's like a non–Star Trek fan hearing the words *Vulcan*, *grups*, and *Spock*. Christian-ese and catchphrases sound like nonsense to those who don't follow Christ.

Finally, Peter denied Christ a third time:

> And after an interval of about an hour still
> another insisted, saying, "Certainly this man
> also was with Him, for he too is a Galilean."
> But Peter said, "Man, I do not know what you
> are talking about." Luke 22:59–60

In other words, Peter's location, where he was from, made him look like he was with Christ. As a Galilean, perhaps he had similar features or mannerisms. Yet Peter, despite being one of Jesus' most passionate followers, denied knowing Him.

Have you ever denied knowing Christ? I certainly have. Perhaps not outright, but when workplace conversations about religion get heated, I don't rush to put on the Team Jesus jersey.

After all God had done for him, Peter denied Him. Jesus could have let Peter drown when he took that leap of faith out of the boat, but Jesus saved him.

He's good at that.

Jesus even told Peter that He prayed Peter's faith wouldn't fail:

> "Simon, Simon, behold, Satan demanded to
> have you, that he might sift you like wheat,
> but I have prayed for you that your faith may
> not fail. And when you have turned again,
> strengthen your brothers." Peter said to Him,
> "Lord, I am ready to go with You both to prison
> and to death." Jesus said, "I tell you, Peter, the
> rooster will not crow this day, until you deny
> three times that you know Me." Luke 22:31–34

As soon as Peter denied Jesus the third time, the rooster crowed. And Peter knew. He knew he had failed, just as Jesus had predicted.

Then Jesus was crucified, died, and was buried.

And Peter thought it was all over.

He thought of the difficulties he had faced while following Jesus, the risks he had taken. Perhaps there were old friends who now shunned him. Maybe his standing in the community was jeopardized. So Peter did something we all do when we lose hope.

He checked out.

Treading: When We Check Out

After His death, Jesus appeared to the disciples by the Sea of Tiberias. However, Peter was discouraged. Perhaps he could not get past his epic failure of denying Jesus three times. So instead of continuing the work of spreading the Gospel, Peter went back to what he knew best—the family business:

> Simon Peter, Thomas (called the Twin), Nathanael of Cana in Galilee, the sons of Zebedee, and two others of His disciples were together. Simon Peter said to them, "I am going fishing." They said to him, "We will go with you." John 21:2–3

Think of what hangs in the balance during that time. Jesus has been resurrected and is about to ascend to heaven to take His place at God's right hand for all eternity. It's one of the most critical times in all of history.

And what does Peter do? He goes fishing. Believing that his sin is too great and his failure is past redemption, he checks out.

How many veteran Christians or leaders do the same thing?

Have you ever, in the most critical time of your leadership or ministry, when everything's on the line and everything seems to be coming together, been so aware of your weaknesses and shortcomings that you simply wanted to escape?

Instead of re-engaging with Jesus, we choose to go fishing. Now, I don't mean literal fishing. I mean physically, emotionally, and spiritually, we go back to the one thing we know best.

Have you ever been leading, but your mind is the one that got away? Teaching, but your mind believes school's out for the summer?

The scary thing when leaders check out and go fishing is that we often take others with us. Just like Peter did. He climbed into the boat to escape and the others chucked in the towel too. But what unfolded is such a beautiful display of God's hydrating grace, love, and mercy:

> They went out and got into the boat, but that night they caught nothing. Just as day was breaking, Jesus stood on the shore; yet the disciples did not know that it was Jesus. Jesus said to them, "Children, do you have any fish?"
> John 21:3–5

"Children"? I wouldn't have used that word if I were Jesus.

Children. That's a relationship term. In that one word, Jesus conveys His willingness to repair the damage. He knew they were stumbling backward in failure and felt ashamed, but He still wanted them.

Has running away mentally or physically ever worked for anybody? Has it worked for a leader or pastor yet? We can't afford any more leaders, pastors, or teachers to check out because they feel ashamed or guilty or inadequate. We've got to assure them of who we are in light of the sheer grace of God: *His children.*

> Jesus said to them, "Children, do you have any fish?" They answered Him, "No." He said to them, "Cast the net on the right side of the boat, and you will find some." So they cast

> it, and now they were not able to haul it in,
> because of the quantity of fish. John 21:5–6

They had seen that scenario before. One of the disciples tells Peter that it's Jesus on the shore. Peter gets so flustered that he puts on his outer garment and then jumps into the water. And when he arrives on the shore, soaking wet, guess who is fixing breakfast?

Jesus.

When we've messed up, we expect retribution, punishment, or abandonment. But that's not what Jesus does. He extends grace and love with sizzling fish over a fire. And even though Jesus asks Peter and the others to bring some of the fish they had caught, Jesus already had fish ready for them to eat.

You see, Jesus doesn't need what we bring to the table. He wants *us*. This Christian journey we're on isn't about need. We were never needed.

We are always wanted.

God's love for us isn't determined by our actions, pedigree, performance, or résumé. In His great love, God desires to hydrate and restore us when we've fallen short and gone backward. He didn't create us because He needed us. He created us because He wants us to be in relationship with Him.

So if you're feeling like Peter today, don't go fishing. Don't check out. Check in with your Savior. You'll discover He's waiting to fix breakfast for you too.

A PAUSE AT THE WELL

Let's take a moment to pause for some practical application.

If you have walked with Christ for any length of time, chances are you've been challenged by fear. We see that in Peter's choice to follow Jesus at a distance after Jesus was arrested.

1. Do you struggle with fear? If so, in what areas?

2. There have certainly been times in my life when I have believed that I would never go backward in my faith. Yet those times happen. Have you experienced something similar? How did that affect your faith walk?

3. If you hold any type of leadership position in your church or the faith community, have you ever felt like going fishing like Peter—not literal fishing, but checking out mentally, emotionally, or spiritually? What was the proverbial straw that broke the camel's back, that initiated "checking out"?

4. How did God draw you back to Himself?

- - - - - - - - - - - - - - - - - - - -
PRAYER STARTER

*Take some time to identify areas in your faith walk
where you have a tendency to check out. Ask God to reveal
the reason and emotion behind each of those situations,
one by one, and confess them to Him. Then ask Him
to remove any shame you may feel and restore your
intimacy with Him.*

- - - - - - - - - - - - - - - - - - - -

CHAPTER 9

A Soldier's Watering Hole

So David set out, and the six hundred men who were with him, and they came to the brook Besor, where those who were left behind stayed. But David pursued, he and four hundred men. Two hundred stayed behind, who were too exhausted to cross the brook Besor. ~1 Samuel 30:9–10

I woke up that morning with only one thought: *I don't ever want to get out of bed again.*

I tried to go back to sleep, but it was too late. Because the film had started.

My brain began flashing moments of the previous day's events like a black-and-white movie. The drive. The courthouse. The bailiff calling order. The lint on my sleeve when I couldn't look up anymore.

I tried to turn it off. Turning my head, I noticed sunlight streaming through the window. Birds at the feeder. A lizard on the lush hibiscus.

The black-and-white film started rolling again. The judge. The pen in my hand. A perfectly round tear splashing on the divorce decree as I signed my name.

It wasn't supposed to end like this, God.

'Til death do us part. That's what we had promised each other thirteen years before. But I never saw this death coming.

I don't know if actual death would have been worse. At least when you're dead, you don't feel anything.

This was too much.

I slid off the half-empty bed to my knees. The sobs came in waves.

Oh God, I can't do this. I don't know how.

In that moment, a single Scripture passage hit me so hard I could hardly breathe:

> It is the LORD who goes before you. He will be
> with you; He will not leave you or forsake you.
> Do not fear or be dismayed. Deuteronomy
> 31:8

My head jerked up; my eyes scanned the bedroom. The verse rang so loud it was almost audible. It repeated over and over, ending in a whisper. Until I understood that I wasn't alone.

I sat cross-legged on the floor and reached for the Kleenex. I needed to be at work in two hours. That thought alone brought a fresh round of tears.

The last four months had taken their toll. Discovering betrayal. Dividing stuff that didn't matter. Believing I would never again smile.

The thought of getting off the floor seemed too great a task. I was just so exhausted. Mentally, physically, spiritually—stick a fork in me because I was done.

Have you ever been exhausted to that degree? When the thought of one more step seems like climbing Mount Everest? Then you need to hear about the brook Besor.

Perhaps you have never heard of the brook Besor. Maybe it's been a while since you read past it in Scripture. But this story needs to find shelf space in the library of God's soldiers. On your bookshelf and mine. At the intersection of exhaustion and rest, this babbling brook runs through the crossroads of two possible futures.

Scripture begins the narrative with rejection. David and his six hundred soldiers have faithfully fought the Philistine war against the Amalekites. One day as the Philistines prepare the next attack, the commanders decide they no longer need David's services. Anger replaces trust as the leaders identify David and his men as Hebrews. Despite a glowing character reference, the Philistine commanders dismiss David and send him and his soldiers packing.

David expresses confusion and anger to no avail. Although they have done nothing wrong, David obeys and steers his men toward home early the next morning. But they don't realize that the Amalekites have taken advantage of their absence. Three days later, David and his soldiers arrive home at Ziklag to find devastation:

> And when David and his men came to the city,
> they found it burned with fire, and their wives
> and sons and daughters taken captive.
> 1 Samuel 30:3

Overwhelmed with grief and loss, they all weep until they can't weep any more.

It isn't long before the men's grief morphs into anger. All heads turn toward David. After all, he led them into battle, leaving their homes and loved ones unprotected. Isn't he to blame? Perhaps he was wrong to entangle himself with the Philistine king to fight against Israel when he left Saul. Maybe some of them remember that David had a chance to kill King Saul in a cave but opted to spare him. As the silent questions and accusations mount, the men's overcharged emotions need an outlet. They label David the scapegoat and start grabbing rocks. The soldiers quickly forget that they chose to leave their homes and follow David. That at one point, they agreed with their leader and chose to strap on their own armor.

Mayhem often sparks short-term memory loss. Mutiny usually follows.

From David's perspective, leaders don't always get to choose their followers. David's men, tired of Saul's tyrannical leadership, switched allegiance to David. Some of the men were the choice best; maybe others, not so much.

And so it is in the Church.

Some are eager to promote the wealth of forgiveness, grace, and love. Others are eager to promote the poverty of blame, guilt, and shame. But what happens when the going gets tough? Pressure has a way of squeezing out and exposing what lies in our hearts.

We love to rally around a victorious leader. When the pastor is doing what we think he ought to be doing and the coffers are full, we'll paint our faces and march in parades. Like when Jesus entered Jerusalem on Palm Sunday. But where were His followers and the frivolity on Good Friday?

Theologian and author Charles Spurgeon spoke to this dynamic:

> We joyfully accept both the cross and the
> crown which go with our Lord Jesus Christ: we

are eager to bear our full share of the blame,
that we may partake in his joy.

When life doesn't go the way we like, picking up stones to hurl
at Jesus, our leader, doesn't solve anything. Leaders make hard decisions and speak truth when no one else will.

When Jesus spoke hard truths in the synagogue in Caper-
naum, many people turned away and no longer followed Him.
But Peter gives the response that needs to be ours when stones
threaten to fly:

> So Jesus said to the Twelve, "Do you want to
> go away as well?" Simon Peter answered Him,
> "Lord, to whom shall we go? You have the
> words of eternal life, and we have believed,
> and have come to know, that You are the Holy
> One of God." John 6:67–69

While David's men fill their hands with stones, David fills his
mind with possible solutions to rescue their loved ones. David
doesn't think of saving his own skin by providing a litany of excuses. Surveying Ziklag's smoking ruins, David's desire for justice
ignites. And he looks up:

> And David inquired of the LORD, "Shall I pursue
> after this band? Shall I overtake them?" He
> answered him, "Pursue, for you shall surely
> overtake and surely rescue." 1 Samuel 30:8

Strengthened by the Lord's assurance of victory, David employs his extraordinary leadership skills. He redirects the men's
anger toward the Amalekites. They drop the rocks, regroup, and
set out to rescue their families.

But they are weary. They still carry the stench and grime of
a long war. The story mentions no meal break, change of clothes,
or even washing their faces. The men set aside their exhaustion in

favor of their loved ones' safety and plunge ahead to hunt down their enemies.

David and his men travel south and reach the brook Besor with its cool, refreshing water. Yet when it's time to remount and move on, two hundred men decide they cannot take another step:

> Two hundred stayed behind, who were too exhausted to cross the brook Besor. 1 Samuel 30:10

How weary does someone have to be to abort the mission to save his loved ones?

Perhaps, as a veteran soldier in God's army, you identify with those two hundred worn-out men. Whether that soldier is you or someone you know, we recognize him. The battleground of the Church is littered with such soldiers.

In the beginning, they stood ground on the front lines, sacrificed, and set the bar for godly service. But now, they're exhausted. Weary. Worn down. They can't even summon the energy to save their own flesh and blood.

Heartbreaking loss can leave you deflated at the water's edge, parched. Addiction can as well. Whatever the reason, church pews overflow with those who have opted out of the latest raging war. You know, those wars that don't have as much to do with how to reach the lost as with what color carpet to put in the sanctuary. Whether to let the choir sing hymns or the worship team lead praise songs.

And as those wars rage, the exhausted, broken, and disheartened litter the water's edge.

As fellow warriors, we must decide what to do with the brook Besor people.

Belittle them?

Ignore them?

Leave them where they've fallen?

David chose the best option: *he let them stay at the water's edge to receive refreshment.* To allow them time to rehydrate at God's wellspring. David marshals the remaining four hundred soldiers and continues the hunt. They come across a sick Egyptian, the slave of an Amalekite, left for dead. They nurse him back to health and gain his trust.

After soliciting vital tactical information from the recovering man, David and his men catch the Amalekites off guard and strike with vengeance:

> And David struck them down from twilight until the evening of the next day, and not a man of them escaped, except four hundred young men, who mounted camels and fled. David recovered all that the Amalekites had taken. ... Nothing was missing, whether small or great, sons or daughters, spoil or anything that had been taken. David brought back all. 1 Samuel 30:17–19

David's label changes from scapegoat to superhero and the celebration begins. They gather up their relieved loved ones, load up all the plunder, and turn back for Ziklag. Eventually, they reunite with the two hundred men who chose to rest at the brook Besor. Some of David's men waste no time in letting their opinion be known:

> "Because they did not go with us, we will not give them any of the spoil that we have recovered, except that each man may lead away his wife and children, and depart." 1 Samuel 30:22

Such a harsh response makes me wonder: is that how the Church responds to those who choose to rest? Maybe we believe that the worn-down have mismanaged their time or resources, not prioritized their schedules or spent enough time in prayer.

Whatever the reason, we accuse.

If that's what we choose, we'll be judging and accusing the rest of our lives. Because the weary are ever present. Spurgeon put it this way:

> There are such in Christ's army at most seasons. We have among us soldiers whose faith is real, and whose love is burning; and yet, for all that, just now their strength is weakened in the way, and they are so depressed in spirit, that they are obliged to stop behind with the baggage.

The returning soldiers' raw words stir a dangerous emotional pot with those who chose to rest. Like an overheated pressure cooker, the explosion could get ugly fast. Everything depends on how David responds.

In the midst of overwhelming pressure, real leaders pause.

Jesus paused in the Garden of Gethsemane. In the face of torture and death, He took a knee to seek His Father's face.

In a leadership-defining moment, David pauses. He turns what could have been his darkest hour into one of his finest. His response tenderizes hardened hearts:

> But David said, "You shall not do so, my brothers, with what the LORD has given us. . . . Who would listen to you in this matter? For as his share is who goes down into the battle, so shall his share be who stays by the baggage. They shall share alike."
> 1 Samuel 30:23–24

Although David made many glaring mistakes during his life, he does not fail to extend grace to the weary. David dignifies the weary solders' decision to rest, making it sound as though their specific assignment included guarding the supplies. He offers the best spin to honor the spun-out.

He could have made those who stayed behind feel guilty. He could have pointed out that the Amalekites might have been much larger and stronger than four hundred men. That they should have known six hundred men would've been better. That perhaps he was worried or afraid at such a possible scenario.

David could have induced shame by reminding them he had sustained the loss of home and family just as they had. That their selfishness added abandonment to his brokenness. But David realized their exhaustion made them incapable of choosing differently. David set an important precedent that day: brook Besor sanctions rest for the worn-out soldier.

Do you find yourself on the roster of the weary? If so, listen carefully: it's okay to rest. Jesus said so:

"Come with Me by yourselves to a quiet place and get some rest." Mark 6:31 (NIV)

Jesus doesn't send us away. He accompanies us. He fights for us when we don't have the strength to stand. He offers us His wellspring of life when our cup is empty.

Your heart may be heavy. Your limbs may be weary. Your doubts may be many, but whatever you are facing, Jesus never abandons you to face it alone. His consistent presence and hydration is your consistent strength and refreshment:

Return, O my soul, to your rest; for the LORD has dealt bountifully with you. Psalm 116:7

In one of the most beloved passages in Scripture, Jesus extends this promise to the exhausted, weary, and dehydrated:

Come to Me, all who labor and are heavy laden, and I will give you rest. Take My yoke upon you, and learn from Me, for I am gentle

and lowly in heart, and you will find rest for
your souls. Matthew 11:28–29

Jesus invites all to rest in Him. He offers us a place at His hydrating well.

Come to Me . . .

Brook Besor also reminds us where the glory rightfully belongs. David and his men had just pulled off a landslide victory. The odds had been stacked against them. David led his men to rescue every single family member of each soldier and all of their livestock and herds. He could have attributed their great victory to skill, commitment, or shrewd tactics. But once again, David sets the leadership standard. He esteemed each man's decision, whether it was to fight or rest, and shares the spoils in equal measure among all. That's grace.

That's what Jesus extended to us on the cross. He didn't weigh and measure each person's accomplishments. All were included in His victory, whether they were faithful disciples or petty thieves.

When the strong gloat over the weary, they forget that one day their muscles will atrophy as well. If you are the strong, focus on the battle, not on who's resting on the bench. One day, you'll need room on that very same bench:

> Every now and then you and I come to turns in
> the road, and many of us are ready, through
> grace, to prove our loyalty by following Jesus
> even when the way is hardest. Though tears
> stand in His eyes and in ours, though we weep
> together till we have no more power to weep,
> we will cling to Him when the many turn aside,
> and witness that He hath the living Word, and
> none upon earth beside. God grant us grace to
> be faithful unto death! Charles Spurgeon

Although this story begins with rejection, it ends with redemption. David became a hero on the battlefield of the worn-out.

So can we:

> We can be in our day what the heroes of faith
> were in their day—but remember at the time
> they didn't know they were heroes. A. W. Tozer

When life leaves us sobbing by the bed, Jesus doesn't abandon us. When the black-and-white film reels of heartbreak, failure, and brokenness begin playing in our minds, we need to take a seat by the brook.

Sometimes we become most exhausted just by trying to stay strong. Are you battle weary today, fellow disciple?

Listen again to His promise:

> *Come to Me, all you who are weary . . .*
> *and I will give you rest.*

Sit down and lean on the Wellspring of Life.

Drink deeply.

Close your eyes, mighty soldier.

Breathe.

Take as long as you like.

The Church needs you.

A PAUSE AT THE WELL

Let's take a moment to pause for some practical application.

1. In your spiritual walk, have you ever experienced a season of such weariness that you couldn't take another step? What were the circumstances?

2. How long did you rest before you felt God restoring your strength?

3. Perhaps you are experiencing that exhausted state right now. He calls us to come to Him for rest. What does rest look like for you?

4. When was the last time you retreated from the world to allow God to restore your soul?

5. Have you ever had a friend or family member stand in your place and take care of things while you rested? How did that affect your relationship with them?

6. When God called you to re-engage, did you feel rested or rushed?

. . . .

PRAYER STARTER

Take some time to sit still for a moment and rest before the Lord. One by one, tell God about those areas in your life where you feel overwhelmed and exhausted, and ask Him to refresh and rehydrate you so that you feel rested when you stand up to continue your journey.

. . . .

CHAPTER 10

PEACE LIKE A RIVER

He makes me lie down in green pastures. He leads me beside still waters. He restores my soul. ⁓ Psalm 23:2–3

Fifty miles inside the Mojave Desert, down an unmarked gravel road, stands a small cinder-block building surrounded by razor wire. Anyone who accidentally stumbles upon the innocuous structure may mistake it for a utility or storage shed.

But outward impressions can be deceiving.

If you were to enter and descend two steep flights of reinforced concrete stairs, a 3,000-pound blast door would welcome you into Terra Vivos, a purported concrete-and-steel solution to the end times.

The vast underground structure was constructed in 1965 by AT&T to protect telephone infrastructures from nuclear attack. In 2010, Terra Vivos promoted the bunker as the world's first everything-proof underground luxury community to protect people and all they hold dear. They claim their facility can withstand a 50-megaton nuclear blast ten miles away, 450-mph winds, a magnitude-10 earthquake, ten days of 1,250-degree surface fires, and three weeks beneath any flood.

Today, they offer a second similar site, not just as a survival shelter, but as a year-round resort and vacation destination. They market it as the ultimate survivalist solution to protect you and your loved ones from harm. There are even restaurants and vehicle in/out privileges. They go so far as to call it a modern-day ark.

Times have changed since the days of Noah, haven't they?

Would you feel safe in such a place? sense true peace? experience freedom from anxiety?

Since I tend to gravitate to wide-open spaces with mountainous, panoramic views, Terra Vivos sounds like a life-draining prison—not a lifesaving option, not an oasis of peace.

By definition, peace is the absence of conflict or other hostilities. Yet our peace we've found in Jesus sustains daily attack. Think back over the past week. Did you experience a day that was 100 percent peaceful?

Me neither.

In those early years as a new disciple, I believed that God would work instant peace in my life. That the garden of every day would bloom nothing but perfect roses. That God would protect my boundary lines and take out hostile intruders with a blast from His mighty nostrils.

Well, He can. But He didn't.

The enemy continues to lie within my borders.

In the Garden of Eden, sin slithered onto the scene to declare all-out war on our peace of mind until the day Christ returns.

Satan employs spiritual guerrilla warfare to launch peace-shattering dirty bombs of doubt at our weak spots. Remember the question that the serpent hissed at Eve?

> "Did God actually say . . . ?" Genesis 3:1

Four words. So much destruction. In that moment, a conflagration was ignited that still burns today, leaving us parched and crispy fried. The tsunamis of fear, riptides of uncertainty, and whirlpools of anxiety drown our peace and leave us gasping for oxygen.

Some days we feel we need survival shelters for everyday life. But who wants life confined to fifty miles inside a desert with no water in sight?

Not me.

I hope you don't either.

Peace comes from God.

The Battle for Peace

Peace. A five-letter word that's so hard to embrace. Peace is a precious commodity given to us by God as a gift:

> But the fruit of the Spirit is love, joy, peace,
> patience, kindness, goodness, faithfulness,
> gentleness, self-control; against such things
> there is no law. Galatians 5:22–23

If peace were processed and traded as a commodity, it would be more valuable than gold. More precious than silver. More sought after than Apple stock.

As busy executives, tired parents, or worn-out volunteers, we sometimes equate peace with being alone. To enjoy self-imposed solitary confinement, so to speak. We dream of no one around to demand a piece of our mind, to consume a bite of our time, or to borrow one thin dime. That familiar scenario of being stranded alone on a deserted island begins to sound appealing when life blurs at a lightning pace.

But we need to be careful what we wish for.

There's a fine line between being alone and being lonely. Being alone is a state of being. Loneliness is a state of mind. One hinges on location, the other on preoccupation. Some people work so hard, climbing the ladder of success, that the peace of God gets shoved off the rungs.

If you're feeling wrung out, chances are you've been reaching for rungs.

But material success can prove to be a hollow victory. I've seen couples who have all the perks—a big house, the latest gadgets, and newest cars—but they can't stand each other because they constantly fight over money.

Peace roots deep in the soil of God's grace.

Peace is being thankful for an overflowing cup instead of filling a bucket list.

The Psalm 23 Solution

The first time I recall reading Psalm 23, it was printed on the back of my grandmother's funeral service folder. Dad's mom was my favorite grandparent, so her death left an indelible impression.

After that day, each time I saw Psalm 23, it reminded me of loss. Of death hovering low. Of women dressed in black, shedding tears that washed off their makeup in streaks.

I didn't associate Psalm 23 with peace.

Still, one of the first things I did as a new disciple was to memorize Psalm 23. Reciting those words by heart made me feel part of the club. That I belonged, somehow.

But over time, and experiencing road bumps of life, God gave me a new understanding.

The dead don't need Psalm 23. It's for the living.

It's for you.

It's for me.

From churches to hospital rooms, in jail cells and across cultural barriers, Psalm 23 has blessed countless millions across generations, homes, and classrooms. Whether in times of peace or tumult of war, those words are the most memorized and memorialized verses in Scripture. They begin with "the Lord" and end with "forever." Just like Genesis, and confirmed all the way to Revelation. Psalm 23 provides a soothing balm for life's stresses.

Why is it so beloved?

In our hectic, addicted-to-speed lives, it provides peace and comfort in the depths of our soul:

> The LORD is my shepherd; I shall not want. He makes me lie down in green pastures. He leads me beside still waters. He restores my soul. He leads me in paths of righteousness for His name's sake. Even though I walk through the valley of the shadow of death, I will fear no evil, for You are with me; Your rod and Your staff, they comfort me. You prepare a table before me in the presence of my enemies; You anoint my head with oil; my cup overflows. Surely goodness and mercy shall follow me all the days of my life, and I shall dwell in the house of the LORD forever. Psalm 23:1–6

Don't you feel more calm and peaceful by simply reading these words?

I know I do!

But they aren't just words. They are God's promises to His children. No matter the strain and pressure of each day, we can close our eyes and find renewed strength in His words. Resting is the key. Without restored souls, we hurl toward hopelessness. When we neglect green meadows, we are plowed under by anxiety. When we pass by still waters, we're destined for the desert.

In short, when we abandon the Shepherd, we are lost sheep flinging ourselves at the prowling lion.

Without Psalm 23, we prepare our own table—devoid of oil and overflowing cups.

Regardless of how far we veer off the paths of righteousness and get tangled in the brush, Psalm 23 provides the assurance that God's goodness and mercy shall follow us every day. But some days, we sprint so fast that we leave goodness and mercy in the dust of our own agendas. We forget to turn around and welcome them, arms opened wide.

This passage speaks universally but touches individually because its real power is in the Shepherd it describes. The familiar, comforting passages of Psalm 23 remind us that the Lord leads us beside His still waters to restore our soul.

He's not out to deplete us.

He's out to fill us with His living water.

The Illusion of Control

Our souls take a beating in this harsh world. And the harsher it becomes, the tighter we try to control every aspect of our life.

Believing we can maintain control is a deadly mirage. God's peace allows us to face uncertainty with the certainty of knowing that He is still in control.

Life is uncertain, but God is not. He still has the whole world in His hands. (Yet another song now ringing through my head.)

Embracing that knowledge as truth, even if we can cling to it only by our fingernails, keeps us from making decisions that further complicate our future.

Jesus understood. He understood our tendencies to attempt control over our own circumstances, so He spoke these freeing words during His famous Sermon on the Mount:

> Which of you by being anxious can add a
> single hour to his span of life? . . . Therefore
> do not be anxious about tomorrow, for tomor-
> row will be anxious for itself. Sufficient for the
> day is its own trouble. Matthew 6:27, 34

Our days will have trouble. But God promises us His peace. The music of God's peace plays across the highest peak and wafts through the darkest valleys in life. It's always playing, begging us to hear God's sweet music of freedom. We will wander with restless hearts after that which provides peace:

> Because God has made us for Himself, our
> hearts are restless until they rest in Him.
> Augustine

When our hearts are restless, it reflects that we have stored our treasures on earth instead of heaven (Matthew 6:19). Moth and rust eat away our peace as we become anxious over worldly pursuits.

God does not want us to live with our minds and stomachs tied in the dehydrating knots of anxiety:

> Therefore I tell you, do not be anxious about
> your life, what you will eat or what you will
> drink, nor about your body, what you will put
> on. Is not life more than food, and the body
> more than clothing? Matthew 6:25

That last sentence struck me like the proverbial bolt of lightning. Talk about an area where we allow anxiety to tie us up in knots!

Two words: **body image.**

Thanks to our culture and media age, women are killing themselves over this peace-robbing, life-scaring issue. Along with millions of women, I have struggled with body image my whole adult life.

Each morning as I step in front of the mirror, I hear it whisper:

Wow, you should NEVER leave the house without makeup. Ever.

That wrinkle wasn't there yesterday. You're getting so old.

You're so fat it's a miracle anyone likes you. You should be ashamed.

Does your mirror whisper too?

My mirror whispers what our peace-destroying culture has programmed my mind to believe about body image—that somehow my physical appearance determines my worth. After all, that's what glossy magazine covers and rail-thin movie stars shout into our homes each day. If you don't have a Barbie figure, Malibu tan, perfect teeth, flawless skin, billowing hair, pouty lips, perky breasts, and endless legs, somehow you are less than. Our culture's obsession with physical perfection murders our self-esteem and mangles the perception of our worth.

Jesus does not value us or love us based on our physical appearance. He didn't sacrifice His life so that we could embrace peace-shattering strongholds. His hydrating, peace-filled truth is this: we are beautiful. Not because the world says so, but because the One who created us says so:

> So God created man in His own image, in
> the image of God He created him; male and
> female He created them. Genesis 1:27

The One who created green pastures and still waters created you. Not because He had to, but because He wanted to. And God does not create ugly.

When you and I look to God for peace, identity, and worth, we will not wander in the parched desert of anxiety. God is still on the throne, and He is in control.

And He promises to restore our soul.

When Fear Comes A-Knockin'

A wail of fear is the first sound we make as newborns when we enter into the world. It is the cry of lost security and familiarity. We can't realize at the time that we'll have to deal with fear for the rest of our lives.

Fear is a force to be reckoned with because it affects us in two ways on two levels. Fear can be a good thing, but it can also destroy us if we try to face it alone. That's why God reminds us:

> Even though I walk through the valley of the shadow of death, I will fear no evil, for You are with me; Your rod and Your staff, they comfort me. Psalm 23:4

Healthy fear is specific and beneficial. For example, when I was a young girl, I was hit by a truck. Had it not been for fear, I might not be here today.

I was coasting down our driveway on my bicycle, looking back over my shoulder at my mom, who was standing in front of the dryer in the garage, folding fresh clothes. As I felt my front tire thump down onto the street, I saw Mom's face change to terror. She let out a bloodcurdling scream and started running in my direction. I whipped my head around in time to see a black pickup truck just feet away. Headed straight for me. Fear triggered survival instincts, and I twisted the bicycle away from the truck to avoid being struck. It would've worked too, if the truck hadn't been equipped with oversized side mirrors for pulling a fifth wheel.

The passenger mirror struck me and catapulted me off the bike. Headfirst into the curb. Ouch. The next thing I remember, I was waking up in our living room with a cool cloth soothing the ugly knot on my forehead. Mom gently applied antiseptic to the scrapes on the side of my face. And a man who was white as a sheet and trembling badly identified himself as the truck driver; he offered nonstop apologies through the tears running down his face.

Had that fear-induced burst of adrenaline not caused me to jerk the bicycle's front wheel, the truck's tires would have run over me, just as they had my bicycle.

I was stiff and had a headache for a few days, an ugly goose egg on my forehead, and concrete burns on my face, but I was otherwise none the worse for wear. Of course I milked it for as long as I could to get out of chores. (Hey, I was a kid.)

Fear is a good thing and mobilizes us into action, almost like a bad storm that passes through. The rains and wind blow hard, but it moves on through quickly.

But unhealthy fear is detrimental. It translates as anxiety because it isn't tied to anything specific; we don't know what it's attached to or what's causing it. It's a shadow and not real. Unhealthy fear immobilizes us physically and hinders our ability to make decisions. It's like steady, cold drizzle that falls for long periods. After a while, our soul starts to mildew, so to speak. It translates into ulcers and high blood pressure.

This kind of fear has more spiritual-type effects because it can be destructive over long periods. Anxiety abides because we can't put our finger on our fear's source, yet we feel it threatening our sense of self.

And that's the key to identifying and surrendering to God our unhealthy, dehydrating fear. We have to *locate* where we have *relocated* our glory. In other words, we try to put our security into something other than God. Something that makes us feel in control or part of how others identify us.

That's exactly what plagued me as a new disciple. I had placed my glory on appearing as a perfect Christian in front of the Church People. I was terrified of losing their approval and acceptance. I had relocated my glory from God to me. I was more concerned about shining the light on my actions instead of on His magnificent face.

It's similar to what a professional ballplayer might do. A healthy fear protects him from dropping the ball so it doesn't cost his team the championship. That's a good thing. But when he retires, he loses his identity, which was tied to the game. He fears that his identity is under attack because his security blanket of image control and security is gone. King David experienced unhealthy fear when he lost his political power, family honor, warrior capabilities, and all the other things in which he had placed his glory on earth (see Psalm 3:1–8).

But when we entrust all of our life—including both our healthy and unhealthy fears—to God, then He promises:

> "Peace I leave with you; My peace I give you.
> I do not give to you as the world gives. Do
> not let your hearts be troubled and do not be
> afraid." John 14:27 (NIV)

Do you want to get rid of unhealthy fear? Follow the smoke of anxiety to the source of the fire. Surrender your misplaced glory to God. Then involve yourself in a community of love.

Love replaces fear.

The opposite of love is fear, not hate. Fear is self-centeredness, while love is self-giving: *"There is no fear in love, but perfect love casts out fear"* (1 John 4:18, emphasis added).

God gives us His shield that surrounds us and protects us in danger. It doesn't protect us FROM danger, but it protects us while the storms of life pound hard.

The answer to overwhelming fear? The ever-present, overarching peace of God.

We don't need the fortified concrete of the Terra Vivos.
We have the Rock of Ages.
The Lord our Shepherd.

CHRIST'S LIVING WATER FOR A THIRSTY SOUL

A PAUSE AT THE WELL

Let's take a moment to pause for some practical application.

1. When you read about Terra Vivos and its claim to offer the disaster-proof shelter to live in, do you find that appealing? Why or why not?

2. When you think over your schedule and demands on your life, do you feel and experience God's peace? Why or why not?

3. Psalm 23 provides refreshment for us in six short verses. Which part of Psalm 23 appeals most to you in this season of your life? What struggles are you facing in that area?

4. If you struggle with control issues, how do you see that play out in your life? What causes you to hesitate to turn those areas over to the Lord?

- -

PRAYER STARTER

Take some time to identify peace-challenged areas in your life. Ask God to reveal the reason and emotion behind each struggle, one by one, and then surrender it to Him, asking Him to provide you with His peace that surpasses all understanding.

- -

CHAPTER 11

GO AHEAD,
DO A CANNONBALL!

"Behold, God is my salvation; I will trust, and will not be afraid; for the LORD GOD is my strength and my song, and He has become my salvation." With joy you will draw water from the wells of salvation. ~ Isaiah 12:2–3

The steady beeping of the heart monitor provided little respite from the droning silence. Tears tumbled silently over my cheeks as I sat beside my dad's hospital bed. Holding his hand in mine, I knew it was the last conversation we would ever have this side of heaven.

For two and a half years, my family and I watched cancer and the effects of its treatment rob Dad of his health, zest for living, and mobility, one test result at a time.

The phone call from my sister had come early on the Monday after Easter: "An ambulance just took Dad to the hospital."

He had been in and out of the hospital several times recently, so I asked my sister if this episode was serious enough to warrant taking off work to drive to Fort Worth from Houston.

She could only whisper her response: "I just hope you get here in time."

I flung clothes and necessities into a suitcase in record time. I called work to apprise them of the situation. I called a neighbor and arranged care for my cats. Within twenty minutes, my suitcase and heavy heart were loaded into the car as I sped north.

The three-and-a-half-hour drive provided plenty of time to think. And remember. And cry. And pray. To relive memories of conversations and fishing trips, Christmas mornings loud with squeals of delight, and horseback rides to watch sunsets when words weren't needed.

And to thank God for an incredible dad.

I went straight to the hospital when I reached Fort Worth to avoid wasting precious time. I'd drop off my bags at Mom and Dad's house later.

And the eight-day vigil at Dad's bedside began.

Mom, my three sisters, and I, along with extended family, turned a corner of the ICU waiting room into our home away from home. We took turns sitting with Dad during the ten minutes allotted for visitors each hour. During those eight days, that ICU corner and the chairs next to Dad's bed became our whole world.

The monitor droned on as I sat memorizing Dad's face. Tears made steady deposits in my lap. Every now and then, despite the ventilation tube down his throat, Dad whispered, "It's okay, honey."

That's one of the things Dad was best at. Offering words of comfort when we were hurting. Whenever life's gales and stormy seas turned us sideways, Dad always stood on deck to stand us upright again.

But I couldn't do that for Dad now. Nothing I could say or do would stand him upright again.

I trusted Jesus with that task.

I leaned in and told Dad once again how much I loved him.

Thirty minutes later, his heart monitor beeped for the last time.

Joy Despite Suffering

Some situations do not naturally lend themselves to joy.

Perhaps your life recently has been one challenge after another and you cannot remember the last time you felt joyful.

But joy is important.

Joy is a source of keen delight, yet it is also an emotion caused by something exceptionally satisfying. To live life to the full, we need a center of joy. Without it, we spend our days simply existing.

Jesus came to give us life—hydrating abundance from His wellspring of life—not merely the capacity to exist:

> "Behold, God is my salvation; I will trust, and will not be afraid; for the LORD GOD is my strength and my song, and He has become my salvation." With joy you will draw water from the wells of salvation. Isaiah 12:2–3

But how often do we trudge through our days watching the clock? mindlessly surfing the Internet, Facebook, or Pinterest?

We tend to scramble from one task to the next on our way toward some vague hash mark on our agenda's timeline without taking the time to enjoy moments. Take it from me—that kind of lifestyle doesn't allow room for joy-filled living.

Joy resides in moments couched in the safety net of salvation. For instance, it brought me great joy to hold my dad's hand and tell him I loved him. Despite the heart-wrenching nature of our circumstances, I knew I would see him again in heaven, thanks to Jesus' sacrifice.

One of the most joy-filled moments I have ever experienced happened during my trip to the Holy Land a few years back. It was sobering to stand at Calvary, but I cannot put into words the joy I felt deep in my soul when we stood inside the empty tomb that Jesus vacated on Easter morning! The Lamb's sacrifice was terrible, but He took away the sin of the world!

Have you spent time recently pondering what brings you joy?

Think about it.

Meditate on it.

Write it down and post it on your bathroom mirror to remind yourself of it every single day.

And rejoice in it!

Scripture reminds us:

> The joy of the LORD is your strength. Nehemiah 8:10

Rejoicing produces encouragement. Reasons to rejoice can always be found.

I realize that some days we cannot muster enough energy to search for it, but it's always present. Even on our saddest days, joy exists. The day my dad passed away was a very sad day for my family and me, but I knew that he was safe in his Savior's arms. No more pain. That joy ember sustained me through the sorrow.

Happiness and joy are different, although we may not make the distinction. Happiness can be a strong emotion, but it is transient. It occurs only when our circumstances are going well. Happiness flees at the first sign of difficulty.

Christian joy is not what the world calls "happiness." The world ties happiness to getting control of our life so we can keep our circumstances favorable. Christians tie joy to surrendering our life to God who has a plan for our life:

> "For I know the plans I have for you," declares the LORD, "plans to prosper you and not to harm you, plans to give you hope and a future." Jeremiah 29:11 (NIV)

The world offers endless advice on how to achieve happiness and maintain it. Out of curiosity, I performed a general Internet search for the word *happy*. I stumbled across a Web site called happier.com where people post pictures of friends, family, places, and things and include a comment as to why the photo depicts something that brings them happiness. It was fun to peruse and read the comments exchanged under each photo.

An older entry offered a list called "Fundamentally Sound, Sure-Fire Top Five Components of Happiness." Here's the list: (1) Be in possession of the basics—food, shelter, good health, safety. (2) Get enough sleep. (3) Have relationships that matter to you. (4) Take compassionate care of others and of yourself. (5) Have work or an interest that engages you.

That's an uplifting list, and there's absolutely nothing wrong with any one of those five things. However, nothing I saw on that Web site would generate the soul-deep joy we need to survive when life blindsides us.

The truth is that we can allow any number of worldly difficulties to hinder our spiritual joy. That's simply human nature. We grumble about who's in the White House, skyrocketing gas prices, and so much more. We all feel the pressures of life.

God knows it's tough being us.

Jesus experienced this life firsthand. There were times when He wept and became angry. But then He would get alone with His

Father. Several times in Scripture, we see where He withdrew to a quiet place to pray.

How often do we follow His example?

When life becomes overwhelming, getting alone with God hits our spiritual reset button with His wellspring of life. It provides the refreshment and rejuvenation that we desperately need on this journey of faith that He's called us to live.

Those quiet places with God provide a safe place to empty our hurt, anger, and frustration to Him. Those times allow Him to fill us up with His peace and joy that we need to make it through the day. Or the next hour.

Or the next test result.

That's one of the reasons I carry earbuds wherever I go. When the world closes in and I begin to dehydrate, I look for quiet places to retreat and turn up the worship music.

Christian joy is unique because it's not based on our circumstantial happiness:

> We rejoice in our sufferings, knowing that
> suffering produces endurance, and endurance
> produces character, and character produces
> hope, and hope does not put us to shame,
> because God's love has been poured into our
> hearts through the Holy Spirit who has been
> given to us. Romans 5:3–5

The apostle Paul understood difficult times. He penned these words along with most of the New Testament while sitting in prison. Would you be able to find joy there? Paul did. Not because of his circumstances, but because his Savior made a home in his heart.

Nero was emperor during the time Paul wrote the Book of Philippians. Nero was a cruel persecutor of Christians who often covered Christians with tar and set them on fire to be used as human torches during his parties. Yet Paul still found reasons to rejoice and stay strong in the faith. In fact, the Book of Philippians is known as the "Book of Joy."

Paul reiterates that a believer's joy does not come and go with our circumstances; rather, it depends wholly on our relationship with the Lord. We rejoice in His promises and in communion with Him. That relationship, nurtured through regular prayer and study of His Word, hydrates us and provides an abiding, deep quality of spiritual life.

As a veteran disciple, have you faced difficult times that challenged your faith?

I've noticed something important about those hard times: God uses the adversity to strengthen my faith.

When life looks vanilla, our faith walk often reflects it.

When those faith-challenging times hit, there's an important distinction we need to understand as God's people:

> Rejoice always, pray without ceasing, give thanks in all circumstances; for this is the will of God in Christ Jesus for you. Do not quench the Spirit. 1 Thessalonians 5:16–19

You and I are to give thanks IN everything, not FOR everything. For instance, I didn't rejoice over Dad's cancer battle, but I rejoiced in the fact that it brought my family together to comfort and love one another through that difficult time.

Every other religion besides Christianity teaches that if we live as we ought, then God will accept us. But if we follow Jesus, we receive God's acceptance and blessing as a free gift of faith on the basis of Jesus' record, not ours. And it is then that we can live as we ought.

Total reversal! To be a Christian is to be someone who is now justified by faith, at peace with God, and accepted by Him.

Following Jesus isn't the path around suffering. It's the only path through it:

> Even though I walk through the valley of the
> shadow of death, I will fear no evil, for You are
> with me; Your rod and Your staff, they comfort
> me. Psalm 23:4

We will walk through valleys, but we never walk alone. And when others around us suffer, we cannot put on pious airs indicating that we might have it all together. That is neither kind nor compassionate. Their suffering provides us a unique opportunity to share the reason that it's possible to rejoice despite suffering: we serve the One who DOES have it all together.

Life can change on a dime. Just ask the parent of a teenager who was killed while texting and driving. Or the child of a parent who suffered an unexpected, fatal heart attack at age 42.

Everything else changes—but not God. Sometimes we need to be reminded of God's stability in our unstable world. In His stability we find joy and happiness, regardless of our circumstances on any given day. We find that kind of joy only in the Lord:

> But let all who take refuge in You rejoice; let
> them ever sing for joy, and spread Your protec-
> tion over them, that those who love Your name
> may exult in You. Psalm 5:11

Satan will do all he can to make our lives joyless, difficult, and problematic. But regardless of our circumstances, we can rejoice.

Through the power of the Holy Spirit we receive the refreshment that God provides from His wellspring of life.

Joy: The Mark of a Christian

Jesus promised the Samaritan woman (and us) that His living water will become in us "*a spring of water welling up to eternal life*" (John 4:14, emphasis added).

The original Greek word for "spring," *hallomai*, refers to "springing up" or "gushing up." That specific reference appears only three times in the New Testament, and the other two times it doesn't talk about water.

It talks about joy!

First there was the lame beggar healed at the temple gate:

> And leaping up he stood and began to walk, and entered the temple with them, walking and leaping and praising God. Acts 3:8

The word used for "leaping" is *hallomai*, a "springing up"!

Then there was the man at Lystra who had been crippled from birth and had never walked:

> He listened to Paul speaking. And Paul, looking intently at him and seeing that he had faith to be made well, said in a loud voice, "Stand upright on your feet." And he sprang up and began walking. Acts 14:9–10

The word used for "sprang up" is *hallomai*. God's joy in us is the wellspring of life. This living water prompts unparalleled JOY because once we have received that drink that God freely gives, eternity is ours.

Isaiah 12:3 confirms that we will draw this water with JOY. This wellspring of life provides the ultimate spiritual fulfillment, not a physical satisfaction. No wonder that promise invokes leaping, joy-filled responses!

Joy should be the unmistakable mark of a believer's life. You and I have been entrusted with the message of the ages. We cannot share it effectively with a long face.

Has a sourpuss Christian ever made a difference in your life?

Mine neither.

Open that joy hose, people, and drench everyone in your path in Jesus' name!

When we are filled with the Holy Spirit, our joy gushes out because His joy is our strength. Not our happiness or circumstances. When we, through the power of the Holy Spirit, realize the bottomless sin debt that we have been forgiven of, our only response is JOY.

The popular Christian author and theologian, G. K. Chesterton said, "Joy, which was the small publicity of the pagan, is the gigantic secret of the Christian."

Joy doesn't have to be a secret! God's hydration in us is a reason for delighting:

> They feast on the abundance of Your house,
> and You give them drink from the river of Your
> delights. For with You is the fountain of life; in
> Your light do we see light. Psalm 36:8–9

Just as an earthly parent delights to see his or her child joyful, the most wonderful blessing we can offer God is to let His love and grace make our hearts glad. Our joy is not arbitrary or random, but is based on two specific things: (1) the promised inheritance of eternity; and (2) the knowledge that there is a reason behind our suffering. God allows trials in our lives to deepen our reliance on Him, expand our faith, and become more like Christ.

Joy is rooted in an abiding faith in God. Romans 10:17 reminds us that our faith is based on hearing the message, through the Word, about Christ. When we read and meditate on His Word, that knowledge develops in us a wellspring of joyful faith.

Perhaps we fall on the opposite side of the spectrum and treat joy as a checklist item.

Got salvation? Check!

Got joy? Check!

But until that checklist travels the eighteen inches from our brain to our heart, that wonderful wellspring of God's truths and promises will never be expressed with joy to those whom God puts in our path every day.

Each morning we have a choice: Will I allow my present suffering to dictate my joy today, or will I choose to shine this little Gospel light of mine despite what I'm going through?

As Christ's disciples and His hands and feet, if we choose to hide our lights under a bushel, then those around us miss out on receiving His joy through us. What if you were the one person God chose to shine a hopeful light into another person's life but you opted out? That other person missed out on receiving that blessing from God through you. But when we serve Him joyfully as the conduit for His wellspring of life, His joy pours into those around us. Where will you pour it today?

So how do we continue to abide in the joy God provides? By clinging to this hydrating, joy-generating truth:

> But God shows His love for us in that while
> we were still sinners, Christ died for us.
> Romans 5:8

So go ahead—do a cannonball into His wellspring of life!

A PAUSE AT THE WELL

Let's take a moment to pause for some practical application.

1. During times when we suffer loss, it's hard to operate in joy. If you have lost a loved one, what did you struggle with most when it came to experiencing God's joy in the midst of it?

2. After reading the differences between happiness and joy, what did that clarify for you?

3. Would those who know you identify you as a joyful Christian? Why or why not?

4. Oftentimes, people equate joy with outward expression. However, joy can look like inner contentment, as well. When you experience joy, what does it most often look like in your life?

* * * * * * * * * * * * * * * * * * * *

PRAYER STARTER

Take some time to identify those areas in your life where you find it difficult to experience God's joy. One by one, surrender your concern and suffering in each area, and ask God to restore His joy there.

* * * * * * * * * * * * * * * * * * * *

CHAPTER 12

EXTREME RAFTING

By this all people will know that you are My
disciples, if you have love for one another.

∽ John 13:35

The morning dawned cold and clear as the large, butter-colored sun rose over the Grand Canyon's breathtaking peaks. Its warmth chased blue mist out of dark crevices.

The aroma of cowboy coffee percolating over an open flame beckoned my fellow rafters and me to gather for breakfast. My inner adventurer sprang to life with eager excitement.

While we chewed on bacon fresh off the campfire, the raft's captain warned us that the rapids awaiting us that day farther down the Colorado River were serious. Not beating around the bush, he stated without blinking that following his orders to the letter could mean the difference between life and death. Our tousled heads snapped to attention as our collective electric shock of excitement dissipated the sleepy atmosphere.

Exchanging nervous glances with my three best friends, I joined our group of twenty-one to pack the gear back on the raft. Then we donned our life vests, climbed aboard, and pushed off from shore.

It wasn't long before the raft began to pick up speed. We could hear the first set of rapids in the distance. In a flurry of activity, each of us double-checked our gear and secured solid footing inside the raft.

Our bodies poised, every muscle tensed as the frothing white water came into view. The captain shouted orders for us to grab the safety ropes and bury our foreheads against the raft.

Exchanging fleeting looks of excitement with my fellow rafters, I flattened myself against the raft and braced as the raft plunged over the rocks.

We hit the frothy white water at full speed, the frigid water causing me to audibly gasp. Woo-hoo!

I felt prepared for anything.

Except for what happened next.

One of the rafters decided she wanted to have a better look at the rapids and did exactly what the captain had warned against—she sat straight up.

At the exact moment, a wave hit her midchest, catapulting her backward into the rest of us. To keep her from going overboard, I grabbed and held one of her legs, while two other rafters grabbed her by the arms and clamped onto her life vest. Excitement turned into fear as we could no longer hold on to the safety ropes with both hands. Half of the rapids still lay ahead. If we let go of our fellow rafter, it might cost her her life.

Somehow we managed to hang on to her and the raft until the captain steered us to safety.

Once we reached smooth water and the danger had passed, the lady gushed apologies and thanks through tears. She was bruised and scared, but otherwise fine. The captain chewed her up one side and down the other, but he was visibly relieved that she had not gone overboard.

I felt relieved that she was all right, but I wanted to knock her lights out for endangering us.

I'm just keeping it real.

A New Perspective

That experience gave me a new perspective.

I wonder how God views the boneheaded decisions in our life. He loves us dearly and wants the best for us, but our choices can cause damage that could have been avoided altogether. Choices impact our daily lives. Whether the choices are ours or not, sometimes they hurt us. Unfortunately, getting hurt is just a part of this crazy ride called life.

Choices are like rocks hidden in the rapids of life. We carefully maneuver through each day, but every now and then, a wall of water hits us midchest or a boulder causes us to capsize.

Before embarking on our Grand Canyon rafting adventure, my friends and I were required to sign liability waivers releasing the outfitters from responsibility should something happen to us—up to and including death. That was a sobering moment.

It's one thing to sign a will, medical power of attorney, or marriage license, but signing a document that sets aside blame because you intentionally choose to put your life in harm's way is entirely different.

That's what Jesus did.

Think about it.

He volunteered to shoulder the sin of all people of all time, and He signed heaven's liability waiver in His blood. His sacrifice released us from the penalty of sin so we could have certain hope of spending eternity with Him.

He didn't hold the Father liable, so the Father held up the Son to be glorified above any other name:

> And being found in human form, He humbled Himself by becoming obedient to the point of death, even death on a cross. Therefore God has highly exalted Him and bestowed on Him the name that is above every name, so that at the name of Jesus every knee should bow, in heaven and on earth and under the earth, and every tongue confess that Jesus Christ is Lord, to the glory of God the Father. Philippians 2:8–11

Jesus proved to be the ultimate extreme rafter, forever saving us from the drowning depths of hell. He went to great lengths, challenging religious leaders, onerous temple laws, and social norms, to reach the people for heaven's gain.

Carrying out Jesus' command to make disciples can be a dangerous calling. Sometimes it looks like catching a flailing person to point them to God's life vest of salvation.

As we raft through life in this lost and hurting world, we're going to get hurt. We're going to get excited in some moments and experience fear in the next. Regardless, Jesus never lets us drown.

He calls us as His disciples, whether new or veteran, and He provides us with His life vest so we can navigate this world's rapids to proclaim His lifesaving love.

Some people may believe they aren't properly equipped to proclaim. But that's a fear-inducing lie of the enemy. The truth is we already have what we need, but perhaps we don't realize its power. In a word, what we need is . . . LOVE.

My grandmother used to have a saying that I believe was pretty common in the South: "I can show you better than I can tell you." Sometimes words get in the way. How we act is oftentimes a more powerful witness than what we say.

Jesus stressed the importance of showing His love to the world by tying our identity to it:

> By this all people will know that you are My
> disciples, if you have love for one another.
> John 13:35

People recognize Jesus through the filter of love displayed in our lives.

How do we point a dehydrated world to the hydration of Christ?

Love.

And just to make sure we know how to demonstrate love, God provides us with a very clear list:

> Love is patient and kind; love does not envy
> or boast; it is not arrogant or rude. It does
> not insist on its own way; it is not irritable or
> resentful; it does not rejoice at wrongdoing, but
> rejoices with the truth. Love bears all things,
> believes all things, hopes all things, endures all
> things. 1 Corinthians 13:4–7

I think it's only fitting to end our journey through this book together by looking at this list that conveys the heart and very nature of God: God is love.

By definition, *love* means having a profoundly tender, passionate affection for something or someone. When we love someone, we want to spend time with them to nurture that relationship.

Love is a verb.

Love *does.*

So how is love communicated?

Love Is Patient

At its core, we can sum up patience with three words: *Patience never pressures.* Love creates as much space and time and margin as someone needs.

Sometimes in our quest to proclaim the Gospel, we get pushy. Don't get me wrong; there is certainly a sense of urgency as we spread the Gospel. But that urgency doesn't need to look like shoving it down someone's throat. No one likes to gag, and we certainly don't want to induce the gag reflex in people when it comes to hearing about God's love.

Love is patient. It never pressures.

Think back to when you first started dating. If your date was constantly pressuring you to either exclusively commit to him or perhaps to push the physical intimacy boundaries, did you really feel loved?

Patience doesn't pressure because pressuring involves backing someone into a corner. We may have the best of intentions when talking with that person we've targeted as our "mission project." But if we're always running our mouths, how can he or she have time to process what he or she hears? Or worse, we become such motor mouths that the person tunes us out completely.

Nobody likes to be pushed, so love must be patient.

What does pressure and pushing look like? For one thing, it looks like too many questions.

Why aren't you . . . ?

Why don't you . . . ?
How come . . . ?
When can you . . . ?

The agenda of love is to love. The agenda of pressure is to force a reaction. Love invites. Pressure pushes.

Patience is developed over time. All followers of Christ have been given patience as a fruit of the Spirit, but it's a fruit that needs time to mature.

Love Is Kind

Sometimes we don't like that word. In our culture, it can convey weakness. This word may provide a clearer understanding: *Love is considerate.*

Being "considerate" means that we take into consideration how the other person feels. In radio terminology, it means we are tuning in instead of broadcasting. In other words, *love listens.*

Relationships flourish when the consideration of listening is regularly extended. When we intentionally listen to what someone is saying, we assign value to that person. Lend weight to her words, importance to her feelings.

Love is considerate.

Love Does Not Envy

Countless relationships have been sacrificed on the altar of envy. Envy, though hard to explain, is easy to spot. Envy's goal is to drag people down. To burst their bubble.

Envy can be as subtle as the "I caught a bigger fish" story. In other words, when someone tells you a story, we feel we have to tell one that's better. Figuratively speaking, someone may tell you he or she caught a two-pound fish. And instead of letting the glory rest with the fisherman, we steal his or her thunder by saying that we just won the local bass fishing tournament with an eight-pound bass.

In Christianity, envy rears its ugly head when disciples like to show how much they know about God—not to point the spotlight on God, but to point the spotlight on their knowledge.

Through such actions, envy hisses, *I don't feel good about myself, so I'm not going to let you feel good about yourself.*

How can you tell if you have an envy issue? Listen to your conversations. If you struggle with envy, your part of a conversation may sound like this: "Oh, that's nothing. Here's what happened to me. . . ." or, "Your problems sound like a dream compared with mine, because I . . . ."

Sometimes we have trouble seeing envy in the mirror. It may be rooted in insecurity, but it's certainly not rooted in conveying God's love.

> A tranquil heart gives life to the flesh, but envy
> makes the bones rot. Proverbs 14:30

Envy thrives on comparison. In God's economy, love and comparison are like oil and water. They don't mix because comparison destroys intimacy. And God desires an intimate relationship with each of us.

Love Does Not Boast

Boasting is another trait that robs God of the spotlight and glory. This one is actually easy to spot because it normally arrives with volume.

Boasting means to speak with exaggeration and excessive pride, usually about ourselves. Normally, the loudest people in any conversation are talking about themselves. Boasting looks like giving ourselves a verbal pat on the back.

Since our mission as disciples is to point people to God and His wellspring of life, how can we point to God if every other word is about ourselves?

Scripture holds boasting in high esteem only when the glory goes to God:

> My soul makes its boast in the LORD; let the
> humble hear and be glad. Psalm 34:2

Boasting and pride go hand in hand since pride constitutes an inordinately high opinion of self. We need to give prideful people room because they won't stand for long:

> Pride goes before destruction, and a haughty
> spirit before a fall. Proverbs 16:18

The Rest of the Love List

Simply reading through 1 Corinthians 13:4–7 provides insight into the heart of God. God is love, and if we are to reach the lost, loving others needs to perch at the top of our agenda.

Love is action, but it's also a mind-set that focuses on grace. When we point others to God's love, He promises to be their shepherd guiding to the streams that give life:

> For the Lamb in the midst of the throne will
> be their shepherd, and He will guide them
> to springs of living water, and God will wipe
> away every tear from their eyes. Revelation
> 7:17

God's compassion and love wipes away EVERY tear. We come in contact with hurting people each day. It's not our job to judge them, it's our job to love them. Holding people close is more important than holding people accountable.

Love forgives and gives. We see that truth clearly in one of the most beloved Scripture passages of all time:

> For God so loved the world, that He gave His
> only Son, that whoever believes in Him should
> not perish but have eternal life. John 3:16

Love gave so that we wouldn't perish.

Everyone deserves to be recognized as a child of the Father, loved by the Son. To whom will you show that hydrating truth today?

A PAUSE AT THE WELL

Let's take a moment to pause for some practical application.

1. Has God ever orchestrated an event in your life that changed your perception of how He views you? What was it?

2. How has that new perception affected your discipleship journey?

3. As you read the list of what love is from 1 Corinthians 13:4–7, do you find it difficult to love others in those ways? Why or why not?

4. God is love. Love is action. Jesus' sacrifice was a clear picture of both. Do you have trouble believing that God sent His Son to die *specifically for you*? Why or why not?

* * * * * * * * * * * * * * * * * * * *

PRAYER STARTER

Take some time to identify those areas in your life where you find it difficult to experience or share God's love. One by one, ask God to strengthen your faith in each of those areas so that you are able to fully embrace His love for you and for others in His name.

* * * * * * * * * * * * * * * * * * * *

EPILOGUE

As Jesus' disciples, you and I will suffer along this discipleship journey, but the will of God will never take us where the grace of God cannot protect us.

Being like Christ means becoming comfortable with being uncomfortable. We need to become comfortable with doing uncomfortable things. It isn't enough to invite people in Jesus' name; we need to strive to make them feel welcome. People feel welcomed by familiarity—knowing that we are a part of the community.

The Pharisees dressed in elaborate garb to set themselves apart. Jesus blended into the community to set God apart. We don't have to bring Christ into a community. He is already there.

Moving. Healing. Transforming.

Transforming the world begins with allowing our lives to be transformed by Christ. But we cannot see Him at work there unless we engage in our communities. Our job is to be the trailer for the blockbuster movie to the hope of eternity.

As with the Samaritan woman, Jesus did not focus on or judge people by their pasts. He focused on how He could change their future. He chose to see our potential.

Christ followers see people for who they can become with Christ at the helm of their lives. When we ask God to remove the world's cataracts from our eyes, we begin seeing people as He sees them.

And when that happens, love comes down.

Jesus is realized.

Living water flows.

> The Spirit and the Bride say, "Come." And let the one who hears say, "Come." And let the one who is thirsty come; let the one who desires take the water of life without price.
> Revelation 22:17

Jesus bore the cost so that entry into His eternal presence would not be based on worldly wealth, position, or prestige, but based on faith alone, that all who believe in Him by hearing His call would not perish but enjoy everlasting life in His magnificent presence.

Say no to the worldly thing to go for the God thing.

Perhaps, like the man near the pool at Bethesda, you've spent your lifetime offering blind, lame, and paralyzing excuses. You liked your mat where it sat. But Jesus lovingly reminds you to get up, surrender those dehydrating excuses, and receive God's soul hydration.

Like Peter, you may have taken your eyes off Jesus when the storm raged. But He will never let you drown. And when He puts you safely back in the boat, I pray that you learn how to worship wet.

Perhaps, like the prodigal son, you have messed up royally. You're hanging your head in shame. Lift thy head, beloved! God your Father scans the horizon, waiting to restore your relationship with Him. I pray that you hear His calling and celebrate the fact that He loves you relentlessly.

Perhaps, like Noah, others criticize you for following God wholeheartedly in ways they don't understand. Although Noah couldn't imagine life beyond the flood, he obeyed God's instructions with single-minded tenacity. I pray that God continues to give you the strength to finish the race, keeping the faith.

Perhaps, like Peter, you are following God at a distance. Observing instead of engaging. You've traded in the Team Jesus jersey for an anonymous seat in the stands. I pray that you hear God calling you back to Him as He fixes you the breakfast of restoration.

Perhaps, like David's soldiers, you find yourself crumpled in exhaustion at brook Besor. Unable to take one more step. You've given until you can't give any more. I pray that you lean against the Wellspring of Life and hear Jesus whisper, *Come to Me, all you who are weary . . . and I will give you rest.* Take as long as you need, valiant warrior.

Perhaps you're wrung out because you've been reaching for rungs. You can't remember the last time you experienced green meadows or still waters. I pray that you allow God to turn your head to notice His goodness and mercy pursuing you. He promises to restore your soul.

So we'll close like we started, beloved.

Jesus shows you to the path to streams of living water because He could not bear watching you shrivel up without hope.

He threw you the ultimate lifeline.

His life was the line.

He doesn't care where you've been.

He doesn't care what you've done.

He cares about *you*.

And He's waiting at the well.

ACKNOWLEDGEMENTS

Listing all of the incredible people who supported and prayed for me as God worked this book through me would fill an entire book in itself. My family and friends, individually and as a group, make this faith journey a true joy. However, there are a few people without whose help this book would simply not have come to pass:

Pastor John Davis, for your friendship, knowledge, and love of God's Word, and your tireless patience in dealing with this theologically challenged blonde. *Thank you.*

Janetta Messmer, for your Ninja editing skills and quirky sense of humor at all hours that improved this book and my disposition by happy leaps and Tigger bounces. *Thank you.*

Pastor Doug Dommer, for your faith-inspiring example of what it means to be a sold-out Christ follower and sharing spiritual wisdom gleaned through God's refining fire. *Thank you.*

Susan Pierce, for countless chats and a plethora of laughs over coffee and a little somethin'-somethin', your openness to discuss issues of faith, and your priceless friendship. *Thank you.*

Luanne Walling, for sharing laughs until we cry, a friendship I can never imagine life without, prayers without ceasing, and shining Jesus by simply walking into a room. *Thank you.*

Rev. Bill Giovanetti, for your spot-on insights on *Sola Scriptura* and sharing your vibrant walk of faith. *Thank you.*

Pastor Mike Mattil, for knowing that life cannot throw at us anything God can't handle. *Thank you.*

Lisa, Sherrie, Lorna, and Kerrie, for your friendship, your love of worshiping Jesus, and letting me pick your brain on the drive to Dallas. *Thank you.*

Peter Burroughs, for making a phone call when weariness almost won. *Thank you.*

The Fab Five, for your prayers, encouragement, and Sunday afternoons of fellowship, laughter, and life gathered around Jesus. *Thank you.*

My Salem Small Group, for enriching my life beyond measure. *Thank you.*

Mom, Lisan, Toni, Monica, I love you more than words can say.

And to my Savior, for calling me out of the boat and catching me when I sink.

SPECIAL ACKNOWLEDGMENT

Rev. John Davis: John is an avid student of God's Word and gifted teacher of Scripture. John received his civil engineering degree from Texas A&M University in College Station, Texas, in 1985. Upon graduation, he received his commission as an officer in the U.S. Navy and served until 1989. Afterward, he enrolled at Concordia Theological Seminary in St. Louis, Missouri, and received his first call to Memorial Lutheran Church in Katy, Texas, for six years, followed by eight years at Immanuel Lutheran Church in Giddings, Texas, and then returning to Memorial in Katy where he now serves as senior pastor.

His extensive experience as a pastor and counselor contributed invaluable insights to this study. I have had the privilege of working with John on the Texas District Lutheran Women's Missionary League for many years. He was one of the first people to suggest that I begin writing, for which I will always be thankful.

Witnessing his contagious love for Jesus, and rapacious passion to dig deep into Scripture has nurtured my spiritual growth, encouraged me to live on God's Word, and step out in faith to write and teach Bible studies. It is a privilege to call him a valued mentor, and to call him and his sweet wife, Brenda, dear friends.

END NOTES

1. C. S. Lewis, http://chroniclesofcslewis.com/465/2014/02/04. Accessed May 20, 2014.

2. Billy Graham, http://billygraham.org/story/suffering-why-does-god-allow-it. Accessed May 16, 2014.

3. John Newton, *The Amazing Works of John Newton* (Alachus, Florida: Bridge-Logos, 2009), 338.

4. http://www.blueletterbible.org/lang/lexicon/lexicon. cmf?Strongs=G910&t=KJV. Accessed November 3, 2013.

5. http://www.wnd.com/2012/06/chariots-in-red-sea-irrefutable-evidence. Accessed October 9, 2013.

REFERENCES

2 Corinthians 1, Logos Research Systems, Libronix, 2007.

Psalm 42, Logos Research Systems, Libronix, 2007.

Achtemeier, Paul J. *Harper's Bible Dictionary*, Harper & Row Publishers, Logos Research Systems, 2007.

American Film Institute, "Dustin Hoffman on Tootsie and his character Dorothy Michaels." https://www.youtube.com/user/afi?feature=watch. Accessed August 20, 2013.

Bible Exposition Commentary, Logos Research System, 2007.

BibleGateway.com, Psalm 42:1–2, Gospel Communications International, ©1995–2008. Accessed March 17, 2013.

BibleGateway.com, 1 Samuel 29–30, Gospel Communications International, ©1995–2008. Accessed October 1, 2013.

Blue Letter Bible. Dictionary and Word Search for baptistēs (Strong's 910). 1996–2013. http:// www.blueletterbible.org/lang/lexicon/lexicon.cfm?page=2&strongs=G907&t=KJV#lexResults. Accessed November 3, 2013.

Blue Letter Bible. Dictionary and Word Search for *baptizo* (Strong's 907). 1996–2013. http://www.blueletterbible.org/lang/lexicon/lexicon.cfm?Strongs=G910&t=KJV. Accessed November 3, 2013.

Blue Letter Bible. Dictionary and Word Search for hypotasso (Strong's 5293). 1996–2012. http://www.blueletterbible.org/lang/lexicon/lexicon.cfm?Strongs=G5293&t=KJV. Accessed January 23, 2012.

Carpenter, Eugene and Philip W. Comfort. *Holman Treasury of Key Bible Words.* Nashville, TN: Broadman & Holman Publishers, 2000, pp. 255, 402.

Coffman, Elesha, "What Luther Said." Article in *Christian History & Biography*, August 8, 2008. http://www.christianitytoday.com/global/printer.html?/ch/news/2002/apr12.html. Accessed October 21, 2013.

Coffman, James Burton, "Commentary on John 4," *Coffman Commentaries on the Old and New Testament*, Abilene, TX: Abilene Christian University Press, Abilene, 1974. http://www.searchsgodword.org. Accessed January 5, 2013.

Coffman, James Burton, "Commentary on Psalm 42," *Coffman Commentaries on the Old and New Testament*, Abilene, TX: Abilene Christian University Press, Abilene, 1974. http://www.searchgodsword.org. Accessed March 17, 2013.

Cooper, Arnie, "The World's First Everything-Proof Underground Luxury Community." http://www.popsci.com/technology/article/2010-09/can-you-save-house-end-world. Accessed August 20, 2013.

DallasNews.com. "Dallas resident, Max Glauben, a Holocaust survivor, lives to share story." http://www.dallasnews.com/news/metro/20130406-dallas-resident-max-glauben-a-holocaust-survivor-lives-to-share-his-story.ece. Accessed August 9, 2013.

Davis, Rev. John, Senior Pastor, Memorial Lutheran Church, Katy, Texas [see acknowledgements].

Giovanetti, Bill, "Sola Scriptura? Five Texts That Compete With Scripture." http://maxgrace.wordpress.com/2013/03/22/sola-scriptura-five-texts-that-compete-with-scripture. Used by permission from the author. Accessed March 22, 2013.

Graham, Billy, http://billygraham.org/story/suffering-why-does-god-allow-it. Accessed May 16, 2014.

Happier.com, "Fundamentally Sound, Sure-Fire Top Five Components of Happiness." https://www.happier.com/. Accessed May 3, 2013.

Henry, Matthew. "Complete Commentary on Psalm 42." Matthew Henry Complete Commentary on the Whole Bible. http://www.searchgodsword.org/com/mhc-com. Accessed November 3, 2013.

Jamieson, Fausset, and Brown Bible Commentary of Psalm 42, eWord Today electronic version. L. Hodgett, 1995.

Kappa Delta Sorority, "Did You Know?" http://www.confidence-coalition.org/statistics-women. Accessed August 20, 2013.

Keller, Dr. Timothy, "Praying Our Fears." Sermon preached on February 5, 2000. http://download.redeemer.com/rpcsermons/tragedy/Praying_Our_Fears.mp3. Redeemer Presbyterian Church, New York. Accessed November 3, 2013.

Lewis, C. S., http://chroniclesofcslewis.com/465/2014/02/14. Accessed May 20, 2014.

Lucado, Max, "Tender Words for the Tired Heart." Upwords, with Max Lucado. http://www.crosswalk.com/devotionals/upwords/tender-words-to-tired-hearts-upwords-week-of-april-9-15-11628653.html. Accessed April 9, 2012.

Mattil, Rev. Michael, "What Can You Handle?", Grace Lutheran Church, Sherman, Texas, sermon preached September 15, 2013.

Mayo Clinic. "Dehydration." http://www.mayoclinic.com/ health/dehydration/DS00561/ DSECTION=symptoms. Accessed August 9, 2013.

McGarvey, J.W. and Philip Y. Pendleton, "Commentary on Psalm 42," *The Fourfold Gospel.* Cincinnati, OH: Standard Publishing Company, 1914. http://www.searchgodsword.org/com. Accessed July 3, 2013.

Newton, John, *The Amazing Works of John Newton* (Alachus, Florida: Bridge-Logos, 2009), 338.

NIV Study Bible. Grand Rapids, MI: Zondervan, 1995, p. 1872.

Pierce, Susan, quoted and used by permission.

Psalm 42, Logos Research Systems, Libronix, 2007.

Scott, Thomas. "Psalm 42," The Treasury of Scripture Knowledge, Blue Letter Bible, 1836.

Slick, Matthew J. "Encouragement." Christian Apologetics and Research Ministry, 1996–2006. http://www.carm.org. Accessed November 1, 2011.

Smith, Judah, "Known", Catalyst Atlanta 2013, live teaching on October 3, 2013.

Spurgeon, C. H., *The Statute of David for the Sharing of the Spoil.* Sermon June 7, 1891, at the Metropolitan Tabernacle, London. http://www.spurgeon.org/ sermons/2208.html. Accessed October 2, 2013.

Stanley, Andy, "Going Public." Sermon preached on January 15, 2012. http://northpoint.org/messages/going-public/. Northpoint Community Church, Atlanta. Accessed January 30, 2012.

Sukkot, "One of the Three Main Jewish Festivals." http://www.jewfaq. org/holiday5.htm. Accessed August 15, 2013.

Thayer's Greek-English Lexicon of the New Testament. Peabody, M.A.: Hendrickson Publishers, 2005.

The Archeological Study Bible, New International Version®, Grand Rapids, MI: Zondervan, 2005.

The English-Greek Reverse Interlinear New Testament, English Standard Version®. Wheaton, IL: Crossway Books, 2006.

The Leadership Bible, New International Version®. Grand Rapids, MI: Zondervan, 1998. Page 1357.

The Lutheran Church-Missouri Synod, "A Statement of Scriptural and Confessional Principles." St. Louis, MO ©1973, pp. 2–7.

The Lutheran Hymnal, St. Louis, MO: Concordia Publishing House, 1941. "All Ye Who On This Earth Do Dwell" 581.

The Strongest Strong's Exhaustive Concordance of the Bible, 21st Century Edition. Grand Rapids, MI: Zondervan, 2001.

Thompson Chain Reference Bible: New International Version®. Indianapolis, IN: B. B. Kirkbride Bible Co., Inc., 1990.

U.S. Geological Survey. "Water Basics." United States Department of the Interior. http://ga.water. usgs.gov/edu/mwater.html. Accessed August 9, 2013.

Vine's Complete Expository Dictionary of Old and New Testament Words. Nashville, TN: Thomas Nelson Publishers, 1996.

Wiersbe's Outline of the New Testament. Logos Research Systems, 2007.

WND.com, "Chariots in Red Sea: Irrefutable Evidence." Article published on June 7, 2012. http://www.wnd.com/2012/06/ chariots-in-red-sea-irrefutable-evidence. Accessed October 9, 2013.

Yom Kippur, "One of the Three Main Jewish Festivals." http://www. jewfaq.org/holiday4.htm. Accessed August 15, 2013.

More from Donna Pyle

The God of All Comfort offers eight lessons based on 2 Corinthians 1:5, "For as we share abundantly in Christ's sufferings, so through Christ we share abundantly in comfort too."

For more information about this Bible study for women, go to www.cph.org. Item 20-3998.

the God of All Comfort

Donna Pyle

Eight Lessons about Hope in Christ Based on 2 Corinthians 1:3–7

A Women's
Small-Group
Bible Study

CONCORDIA PUBLISHING HOUSE · SAINT LOUIS

Published by Concordia Publishing House
3558 S. Jefferson Avenue, St. Louis, MO 63118-3968
1-800-325-3040 · www.cph.org

Text © 2012 Donna Pyle
Illustrations © Shutterstock, Inc.

Manufactured in the United States of America.

1 2 3 4 5 6 7 8 9 10   21 20 19 18 17 16 15 14 13 12

Thank You...

To *Luanne*, for giggles, accountability, loving Jesus outrageously and contagiously, and showing me how.

To *Doug*, for sharing your sideways humor, leading with a servant heart, and allowing God to redeem and use your broken pieces to profoundly impact my life.

To *Kristin*, for gracefully asking tough questions that God used to heal my heart.

To *Joel*, for intense integrity, speaking the truth in love, and letting your yes mean yes.

To *Roxanne*, for standing in faith instead of falling in fear.

To *Jennie*, for ending your sentences with exclamation points and making a difference in my life and the lives of children.

To *Hannah* and *Ashley*, for letting hope and the love of Jesus shine so brightly in and through you.

To *Heather*, for your amazing blog and insights on addiction and grace.

To *Lindsey*, for your tender heart, passion to follow Jesus, and grace-filled care of those you love.

To *Ray*, for sharing honest feelings with compassionate grace.

To *Janetta (Hoot)*, for your ninja editing skills, wicked humor, and boundless encouragement.

To *Sherrie, Lisa, Annie,* and *Bre,* for belly laughs, gut-level honesty, Starbucks runs, loving Jesus tenaciously, and enriching my life beyond measure.

To *Salem's worship planning team,* for your invaluable input and servant hearts.

To *Rachelle,* the best literary agent on the planet.

To *The Coolios,* the most amazing community of Christian writers, for your hearts like Jesus, writing expertise, and calming words when God turned me upside down writing this study.

To *Lisan, Monica,* and *Joni,* the most amazing sisters and best friends I could ever ask for.

To *Mom,* for lavishing on me unconditional love and compassion so much like Jesus.

And most importantly, to *my Savior;* my life would be rubbish without You.

Table of Contents

Forward

Christmas decorations hang forgotten. Wheezing cats snooze nearby, whiskers and paws twitching. Fingers type a staccato beat into the night. The keyboard's M is barely visible from wear. Soft music breaks the loud silence. The fireplace blaze reduces to embers as the dramas unfold.

As I complete writing this Bible study, I'm thanking God for this privileged loneliness. This self-imposed solitary confinement is necessary to translate interviews revealing soul-scarring events. Essential to capture. Difficult to articulate.

Theirs and mine.

The history of real pain. The drama of spiritual struggles. Stories of anger, misplaced expectations, fear, abuse, loss, and betrayal. They shout for space on the pages.

And God whispers into the chaos.

Comfort.

Bruised lives redeemed by a faithful Healer. Hope offered by a murdered Messiah. Restoration secured by a risen Savior. "For as we share abundantly in Christ's sufferings, so through Christ we share abundantly in comfort too" (2 Corinthians 1:5).

No one likes suffering, yet there's healing in the telling.

Abundant comfort.

As the laptop screen glows long into the night, gratitude overflows as I recall the faces of these story-sharers. The profound impact they've had on my spiritual journey. Honored by their trust to reveal great pain redeemed by an even greater God. A holy experience. And I'm already praying.

For you.

For the lives He will touch by these studies written around their stories in light of His Word. For the shadowed hearts He will usher back into His glorious light through them.

And somewhere in these stories, I pray you find yours.

Pouring amazing grace through the chapters, God gushes His love into our empty wells. Faithfully demonstrating how His life-giving Word works healing in us. Received, His soothing comfort then offered through us. Despite our discomfort.

If we let Him.

Introduction

In the midst of suffering, comfort often surprises us. A kind word. A soothing hug. A special delivery of the Savior's love. Right where we stand. Right when we get blindsided.

In the middle of hurt.

On the main street of chaos.

In the vortex of life's storms.

We all need comfort and compassion because life gets tiring, does it not? When we struggle with sin, when family members aren't saved, when bills stack up unpaid, work exhausts us, our health fails, and loved ones hurt.

Discouragement easily seeps in.

God desires something infinitely better for us. Nothing touches our lives that He has not filtered first. But discouragement robs us of peace and contentment. If it hangs around long enough, doubt, despair, and depression join the pity party.

Suffering causes us to forget our blessings and look only to our circumstances—especially if we suffer over a prolonged period of time. It creates distaste for the present. Dissatisfaction with the past. Distrust of the future.

But when we view our difficulties from the balcony of faith, we rest in God's assurance that He never leaves us unloved or uncared for. God's hope shines as a beacon of comfort.

Hurt blinds us to yesterday's blessings, causes indifference to today's opportunities, and creates insecurity regarding tomorrow's provision.

Over these eight lessons, our journey will take us through a section of Scripture titled "The God of All Comfort," in 2 Corinthians 1:3–7. The apostle Paul, the author of that letter and an expert when it came to suffering, offers insight and encouragement that God is not blind to our troubles.

God is also not necessarily concerned about our comfort, at least the way you and I define it. He's concerned about our character. So to burn off the dross, He hands us the blast goggles of His Word and lets loose His refining fire in our lives. He burns away pride, ego, arrogance, self-centeredness, and everything else that inhibits His work in and through us.

Some days we feel crispy fried. Other days, we find hope and renewal shooting up green through a scorched heart.

In order for us to be able to relate to comfort from many different scenarios, I interviewed seven faith-filled Christians who relied on timeless truths to walk in obedience despite loss and heartache. Through their stories and God's amazing Word, we follow the unmistakable footprints of a loving Savior who turns scars into life-changing stories.

This handful of ordinary people originate from very different backgrounds, yet use their extraordinary experiences to shine a God-sized floodlight on a compassionate Savior who weeps when we weep.

Let me warn you, these stories aren't pretty. Loss, betrayal, shattered trust, anger, misplaced expectations, abuse, cancer, fear, divorce, and sacrifice bleed onto these pages. Followed quickly by love and hope provided by God, who relentlessly pursues us with ultimate comfort.

We need the God of all comfort.

As these stories unfold and we dig deep into Scripture together, God's encouragement pours over us as we behold time and time again how He moved, rescued, and restored good from bad.

God redeems our stories through His story.

If you have suffered, needed comfort, and craved compassion, this study is for you. Over these eight lessons, you will learn about a Savior whose mercies arrive new every morning. Comfort that surpasses what our eyes see. Compassion offered by One who suffered most of all.

This study will encourage you.

You may be going through a difficult, painful storm in life right now. You might be resting in the calm following one. You may see storm clouds on the horizon. But pain is a chapter, not the book. In the midst of pain, God engraves His love on your softened heart as He adds your story to His history of faith-filled warriors.

You may feel a sense of hopelessness in your situation, but God reminds us that we have hope and a future with Him. As we study these Scripture passages about comfort, grace, and love, God whispers reminders into our souls of His promise to bring good out of every situation. Even the one you're experiencing right now.

This study will challenge you.

Perhaps you could offer college-level classes on comfort because you strive to maintain it at any cost. You don't like risk. Life is vanilla. Comfortable. Safe. You've traded your position on the spiritual battlefield for an observer's box in the stands. You dodge the fiery darts of spiritual warfare, hiding behind those actively engaged. You don't care who gets hit. As long as it's not you.

God wants more for you.

This study will re-ignite your passion.

Perhaps life has dealt you so many painful blows that you've given up. You've checked out of relationships. You've stopped going to church. You see the negative side of every situation first. You don't remember what joy feels like.

Yet Jesus pursues you in love. A Messiah who died so you could live fully alive.

This study will change your focus.

You may be angry with God because you cannot figure out the reason for your pain. You've been good. Lived an upright life. Served Him faithfully. Tithed and given generously.

But instead of allowing God to guide your situation, you focus like a laser on one question: *What can I do to make things better?* Self-centered, works-based focus has closed your mind to the unconditional love and purposes of God.

God-based focus strengthens us. When our spiritual eyes rest on Him, we receive His guidance and comfort. He enables us to offer encouragement to others. Helping those around us takes our eyes off of our troubles. We receive His comfort so it flows through us to those who hurt.

Keeping our eyes on Jesus is key.

FATHER OF MERCIES

Even in the Fire

Blessed be the God and Father of our Lord Jesus Christ,
the Father of mercies. 2 Corinthians 1:3

When the uniformed officer pulled into her driveway, Jennie knew time was up.

How could 20 minutes have gone by so fast?

That's all the warning she'd received. And it had expired. She had to leave.

Now.

She and her two daughters haphazardly packed the minivan with all the worldly possessions they held dear. There wasn't time to be neat or organized. The danger raged closer. Mandatory evacuations had been ordered. For the first time in her life, she was fleeing to save their lives. It just seemed so surreal. Thick smoke choked out the midday sun. Huge flames appeared in the distance. The sound of exploding pine trees jolted her senses. Smoldering ash carried on high winds forewarned a deadly scenario. The Texas wildfires were out of control, destroying everything in their path. The lethal inferno headed directly for their home.

How do you prioritize your life in twenty minutes?

Jennie struggled to focus through panic and fear. She called her brother-in-law to enlist much-needed guidance. She needed to organize her things. Grab important papers. Call a friend to ask for shelter. Find both cats, who had disappeared under the beds when they sensed chaos.

And the whole time she prayed: *Lord, please help us. Preserve us. Protect those trying to save us.*

Reminding herself to walk with purpose instead of run in panic, she gave her daughters urgent instructions. Twenty minutes seemed to go by in seconds. But when the officer arrived, she had to leave immediately, whether or not she had grabbed everything they needed. They rushed out the door and flung themselves into the minivan. The dense smoke blanketed the sun in an eerie red glow.

It looked like hell had taken over.

The policeman shouted for Jennie to leave. He had to warn others, corral panicked livestock, block roads, and direct approaching firefighters. As she slid the key into the ignition, she met the eyes of her daughters. The anxiety reflected there matched her own. With a reassuring look, she backed the minivan down her driveway.

Jennie, Hannah, and Ashley didn't know if they would ever see their home again.

They arrived safely at her friend's home and settled in for the night. Jennie just kept praying: *God, please find a way to let me know one way or the other if my home is still standing. I cannot bear not knowing.*

She slept fitfully. Rising early, she wandered into the kitchen. Her friend was listening to the news as she made breakfast for them. Jennie sat down at the kitchen table as thoughts bombarded her mind. *What next?*

She turned toward the television and froze.

The news reporter stood in the middle of charred remains, relating the destruction caused by the wildfires. But Jennie's eyes were riveted to the swing set in the background.

That's ours! It's not burned!

Joy began to fill Jennie. Then the camera panned out. Where her house should have stood there lay piles of ash. Pieces of metal. Fragments.

O God, help us. Thank You for finding a way to let me know. But—now what?

Although the massive fires affected thousands of lives, it felt personal to the core.

Difficulties always do.

Where do we find comfort when our world turns upside down?

We desperately need the Father of mercies in that moment.

Day 1

REFINING FIRE

Emotions feel raw after such a traumatic event, so Jennie emphasized to her daughters that they were facing this as a team. They would deal with whatever came along as a team. And they were moving forward as a team. One day at a time.

Have you ever known people with the ability to comfort others despite personal tragedy? They face seemingly overwhelming odds or heartbreaking loss with a calm demeanor and purposeful steps. As we look on in amazement, we wonder at their secret.

On the other hand, some people feel devastated by personal hardships. They find no peace or consolation as they fall apart at the seams.

Where do those comfort givers find the strength to move past their suffering?

The apostle Paul was one individual who learned that secret, and he passed it along to us in his second letter to the Corinthians.

1. With what words does he start out in 2 Corinthians 1:3?

_____

_____

Although Paul experienced great suffering, persecution, and opposition in his ministry, he begins the letter by praising God. Paul realized that even in the midst of hard times, God, who brings grace and peace, is worthy of our worship.

2. When you face difficult times, are you still able to praise God?

_____

_____

3. What does offering God praise look like in your life?

_____

_____

Rather than starting with the problem, Paul begins 2 Corinthians 1:3 by identifying the Problem-Solver: "the God and Father of our Lord Jesus Christ." Paul never shunned God's refining fire. When he struggled with a personal weakness—a thorn in the flesh—he still affirmed God's faithfulness with a thankful, worshiping heart. With tenacious faith, he relied on God's promise to provide guidance and strength for his times of trial.

4. When you endure trials, do you rely on God as tenaciously as Paul did?

_____

_____

You and I operate in a very capable culture. Advances in technology place the world's information at our fingertips. When we experience difficulties, we're more likely to turn to computer search engines for a quick answer instead of patiently waiting on God to provide guidance and direction.

But computers cannot provide us the strength to endure.

The grace to be kind.

A love that forgives.

When trials exceed our spiritual or emotional capacity, search engines offer cold companionship. Instead, we need to swallow our pride and learn dependence on God. When we trust God and His leading, we receive His comfort.

5. How do these verses demonstrate living a life dependent on God?

2 Chronicles 14:11

_____

2 Corinthians 1:9

_____

Second Corinthians is an intensely personal letter from Paul. False teachers had levied attacks against his character and the integrity of his ministry, so he used strong words to defend, correct, and teach. Yet he did so with great compassion. He wrote 2 Corinthians out of a godly love for those who had gone astray. Compassion represents a vital ingredient in establishing relationships.

6. According to Isaiah 54:10, what two things does our compassionate God say will not be removed?

_____

_____

God's covenant of peace and steadfast love brings us comfort. From a human perspective, showing compassion most often occurs up close and personal—in our space, so to speak.

Compassion is something we _feel_.

Comfort is something we _do_.

One cannot be genuine without the other. Relationships become uniquely important in our times of suffering because we receive comfort and compassion at a deeper level from those who know us best.

If you are enduring a difficult season now, translate that to your own situation for a moment.

7. Are you more open to receive comfort from a close friend or an acquaintance? Explain.

_____

_____

An acquaintance may attempt to comfort you, but her words ring hollow. They have little effect because an acquaintance does not know you well enough to be genuinely concerned.

Conversely, some people may feel compassion but cannot move past their own pain or problems to offer comfort to others. They listen to others' difficulties and immediately launch into an explanation of how their suffering is much greater.

You and I serve as vessels of God's compassion. Self-centeredness blocks the flow of God's comfort to those around us in need of it. When we take our eyes off of our own issues to help those who are hurting, it brings our situation into perspective. Comfort often takes the form of a listening ear, soothing words, hugs, and a handkerchief offered to tear-stained cheeks.

8. Take a moment to recall an act of compassion you have received that stands out in your memory. How did it cause you to feel?

_____

_____

9. Did it change how you felt about the person who offered it?

_____

_____

If our hearts overflow with compassion over the hurts of others, just think of how much our heavenly Father's heart is filled to overflowing with compassion and love for His beloved children.

Deuteronomy 4:31 tells us, "The LORD your God is a merciful God." God's amazing compassion is backed by action. He loves us too much to allow us to perish in our sin. In fullness of compassion, He provided His Son as the atoning sacrifice.

10. What attributes of God are mentioned in Exodus 34:6?

_____

_____

Compassion, grace, love, and faithfulness merely scratch the surface of God's goodness.

Paul showed compassion on God's people in Corinth because of deep love. Jesus had died for them, too, so Paul esteemed them by speaking the truth in love. But rather than beating them over the heads with facts, he used compassion and love to convey God's truths.

In the days following the fire, Jennie and her daughters received an avalanche of compassion—phone calls, text messages, gift cards, furniture, and more. Each day brought new and amazing blessings, and they still marvel over each one.

Today, Jennie and her daughters have a new home, and they work together to build their future as a family. They share a special bond that formed when God's refining fire touched their lives. Each day, they look for and discuss the amazing ways Jesus blesses them *that day*. Jennie never wants to take God's provision and comfort for granted. They talk about how to pay that love and compassion forward.

With the comfort of Jesus working through their hands and the love of God speaking through their lips, they jump at the opportunities to help others facing difficult times.

Blessed be the Father of mercies.

Day 2

ADOPTED IN LOVE

Long before the fire consumed Jennie's home, a different fire consumed her heart. Although not married, she longed to offer a stable home to children.

As a teacher, Jennie had seen many children exhibit serious behavioral problems, relational difficulties, or poor performance in school because they did not have a stable home life. So she began to pray about how she could help. God soon put the desire in her heart to adopt. But not to adopt just any children—God prompted her to adopt older girls who had been trapped in the foster system for years. More-difficult, troubled young girls, not moldable, newborn babies.

These girls would have behavioral issues. Abandonment scars. Destructive habits. *Fear of trust.* Jennie knew God was calling her to show compassion, demonstrate unconditional love, and provide a good home for these girls while giving them a chance at a normal life. Trusting the Father of mercies, she moved forward toward His calling for her, trusting Him to fill in the gaps.

1. Have you ever followed through on a calling from God when you couldn't see the end result? What happened?

_____

_____

2. What did God show you in the process?

_____

_____

Adoption brings a sense of belonging. A family to call your own brings an enormous sense of comfort.

3. What does Ephesians 1:5 say about our adoption by God?

_____

_____

God *predestined* us, which means He intended to adopt us from the very beginning of the world. Before you were born, He chose you to live with Him in eternity. God has adopted us as sons and daughters, along with all that implies, through baptismal water and the power of His Word.

4. Since we have been adopted, what titles does God bestow on us?

Ephesians 3:6

_____

Romans 8:16

_____

1 John 3:2

_____

Just as Hannah is part of Jennie's family, you and I are part of God's forever family through adoption. That truth fosters unending comfort from the inside out. As God's people, we are not just randomly gathered as a generic flock. We have undergone spiritual adoption into the family of God.

5. What do the following verses tell us about our adoption?

John 1:12–13

_____

Romans 8:15–17

---

2 Corinthians 6:18

Galatians 4:5–6

Hannah and Ashley rarely experienced compassion or comfort before Jennie adopted them. Both arrived on her doorstep, a few years apart, jaded by years of being shuffled through the foster care system. They were concerned only about their own interests, fiercely guarding what was theirs. They shared belongings through gritted teeth, following fierce arguments. They marked out their territory and defended it.

Over time, as Jennie faithfully took them to church, God began softening and mending their hearts. Hannah said:

> Before the fire, I didn't have the relationship with Jesus that I do now. I constantly kept track of what I gave to be sure I received in return. I never felt contentment. I saw the awesome relationship my mom had with Jesus, and I wasn't acting like that. I see now that God used the fire to get my attention. Now I can see more and more what I can do for others instead of myself. I don't count my life by the man I'm going to marry or the number of children I want to have. It's about who I can help today.

Trials by fire, both physical and spiritual, tend to change us from the inside out. Fires that change more than our address.

Refining fire that changes the landscape of our hearts and ushers in new life.

But God, the Father of all mercies, pours comfort like salve on the wounds. Just think about the apostle Paul. Formerly known as Saul, he committed horrendous crimes against Christians.

6. According to the following verses, what did his life look like before Jesus met him on the road to Damascus?

Acts 8:1–3

Acts 9:1–5

We may tend to believe that someone like Saul does not deserve the comfort of the Father of mercies. Yet, although you and I likely have never committed such crimes, aren't we just as guilty?

Guilty of judging.

Persecuting by gossip.

In the fullness of compassion, Jesus voluntarily died so we could live.

Today, Hannah is a well-adjusted, beautiful, 14-year-old piano player. Ashley is a lovely, dynamic, 13-year-old student. They both love Jesus and know that He saved them from a very difficult foster life.

They have experienced adoption. So can you.

God, our Father of mercies, offers us ultimate comfort through the transformative, refining fires in our lives. Adoption into God's family provides an eternal home for all who surrender to Jesus as Lord.

Comfort without end.

Blessed be the Father of mercies.